THE **DEPARTMENT** OF
HOMELAND DECENCY

**DECENCY RULES
AND REGULATIONS MANUAL**

THREE RIVERS PRESS • NEW YORK

Published in the United States by Three Rivers Press, an imprint of the
Crown Publishing Group, a division of Random House, Inc., New York.
www.crownpublishing.com

Three Rivers Press and the Tugboat design are registered trademarks of
Random House, Inc.

Originally self-published in different form by Frankensue Books, St. Paul,
Minnesota, in 2006.

Library of Congress Cataloging-in-Publication Data
Fuller, Susan, 1950–
    The Department of Homeland Decency : decency rules and regulations
manual / Susan and Frank Fuller. — 1st ed.
    1. Conduct of life—Humor.   2. Ethics—Humor.   3. Totalitarianism—
Humor.   I. Fuller, Frank, 1949–   II. Title.
    PN6231.C6142F85 2008
    818'.5402—dc22

                                                            2007027622

ISBN 978-0-307-39408-8

Printed in the United States of America

Design by Ruth Lee-Mui

10 9 8 7 6 5 4 3 2 1

First Three Rivers Press Edition

If you think you have witnessed indecency,
you probably have.

[CONTENTS]

SECTION VIII: HOMELAND FUN AND LEISURE
*The slippery slope that can lead from fun to "fun." How long
can you sit and relax in a chair before you get indecent urges?
Why do men tinker and women don't? How do gun racks fit into
the camping experience? Are there archaeological digs that tell
the true story? What about Branson?*   111

SECTION IX: THE GLOSSARY OF INDECENCY
*A preliminary listing of indecent words, their definitions, and
accepted DOHD synonyms. It is preliminary because new words
are being added all the time. Homelanders will be expected to
update this current glossary with all the new bad words. This
section should not be read by children or weak adults.*   125

APPENDIX A: PROSCRIBED PUNISHMENTS   135

APPENDIX B: STARTING YOUR OWN
NEIGHBORHOOD DECENCY POSSE   141

APPENDIX C: FUND-RAISING FOR HOMELAND
DECENCY   161

APPENDIX D: HOMELAND EXTRA-INTERVENTION   169

You have nothing to fear
if you have nothing to hide.

You have nothing to hide
if you have nothing to fear.

So fear nothing
and you need not hide.

Hide nothing
and you need not fear.

WHAT IS THE USA DECENCY ACT?

The **USA DECENCY ACT** (**D**eny **E**volution, **C**ombat **E**urope, and **N**ever, ever **C**oncede that **Y**ou might be wrong about anything, anytime, ever) was passed this year by an overwhelming majority of your decent Republican and enlightened Democratic congressional representatives and senators. Decency is now the law of the land. You are required by law to be decent. So are your relatives, friends, neighbors, and coworkers. There will be no exceptions.

Furthermore, the **USA DECENCY ACT (UDA)** established a new federal department, **The Department of Homeland Decency (DOHD)**, whose duty is to enforce all regulations, alerts, and punishments of the UDA. Its primary goal is to foster and promote the Age of Decency in the Homeland as quickly as possible by rewarding the decent and punishing the indecent.[1]

A TRADITION OF DECENCY

DOHD historians looked at Homeland history and realized things were a lot better a long time ago. Back then, life was decent.

Men worked all day without overtime or Social Security. They were fit and strong and paid their debts on time and didn't go to government offices for handouts if they lost their jobs or were injured while performing them. They raised large families with their wives and didn't expect others to pay for their health care. Good and decent, they lived their decent lives to the fullest, until one day—from God-given exhaustion—they would fall over dead. They didn't linger, whine, or sue anyone over the unfairness of it all. They just dropped dead and went on to their eternal reward.

Their wives were just as decent. They stayed home and cooked and cleaned and made themselves look pretty for their husbands, just as our Intelligent Designer intended them to do. They did not complain about their numerous household and child-rearing duties. Nor did they ever find anything but joy in being pregnant over and over again. And when their men fell over dead suddenly, leaving them no pension or bank account,

[1] Who are by definition terrorists, foreigners, gang members, radical students, professors, sluts, hedonists, secular humanists, and college professors, or any combination of those or anyone else DOHD may decide are opposed to indecency.

they didn't go to the government expecting money for nothing. They took in sewing to make ends meet, all while raising their children to become decent, hardworking, noncomplaining adults.

The children of these decent parents grew up to be decent. They did what they were told, spoke only when spoken to, and didn't pierce their body parts. They understood they could be spanked repeatedly because it was their parents' right and obligation to do so. Spanking, when administered through the benevolent authority of a decent man, always turned children into decent adults.

WHAT WENT WRONG?

But something happened in the Homeland. The Sixties. The liberal media. The Kinsey Report. Rock and roll. The Pill. Men getting in touch with their feelings. Women going to work. Women wanting to make the same amount of money as men. Women burning their bras. Actors doing "it" in the movies.[2] Children being educated about "it" in school. Free love. Free the whales. Naked is beautiful. And activist judges allowing it all to happen.

The Homeland had run amok, and the few remaining decent people, afraid to stand up and be proud of their decency, went underground.

---

[2]It is too indecent to discuss what "it" actually is, but we know you know what we are talking about. We at the Department of Homeland Decency think this is the best way to deal with this mature subject.

RETURNING TO DECENCY

But now, DOHD and the UDA—especially after 9/11—are empowering these decent Homelanders to bring all that was decent back to the future. The following are the basic DOHD goals, which will be explained in greater detail in later sections of this manual.

APES ARE APES. MEN ARE MEN. All schools will teach this. Sound science in Kansas has proven that what separates us from apes is our sense of decency: Apes don't fight to liberate other countries of apes and apes don't have faith-based programs to help less fortunate apes. Ergo: We don't come from apes, we are better than apes, apes are nothing like us, and those who teach otherwise will go to prison.

MEN ARE MEN. WOMEN ARE WOMEN. Families need Mommy taking care of the home and raising the children while Daddy does the hard and important things outside the home. Mommy must also use her femininity to keep Daddy proud that he is a man and happy that he isn't a woman.

NO MOMMY-MOMMY OR DADDY-DADDY MARRIAGES. Sound, decent science has proven that people's body parts fit together only when a Mommy and a Daddy do "it." They don't fit together when other combinations do "it." Unnatural "it" is indecent, disgusting, abhorrent, icky, and thus filled with unnatural and indecent moaning and grunting as parts that don't naturally and decently fit together are forced to fit together in indecent ways.

CLOSETS ARE GOOD. Our Homosexual Friends (**OHFs**) should remain in closets with other homosexuals. "Don't Ask, Don't Tell" will be expanded to "Don't Ask, Don't Tell, Pretend the Closet Is a Small Apartment."

MUSIC WILL SOOTHE THE SOUL, NOT AROUSE LUST. Lyrics will praise religion, love, simple hand-holding, and war heroics. Melodies will be soft and appropriate as background in all elevators, shopping centers, and restaurants. Singers must be able to sing like Celine Dion or play an instrument like Kenny G. Lyrics must be understood by everyone.

LUNCH IS NOT FREE. One hundred years ago, there were no free lunches. Being able to make it without a handout is a sign of a healthy, decent Homeland. No one should expect a handout unless they can prove to a faith-based charity organization that they will work to become decent, productive, and supportive of the Homeland.

NUDITY BELONGS AT HOME IN THE BEDROOM IN THE DARK. Books, television, magazines, and movies will no longer feature the unclothed. There is one exception: Women in television commercials may continue to be depicted curvaceously and alluringly while clad skimpily when selling a product that will make the Homeland stronger (e.g., SUVs, beer, sports equipment). This will keep Homeland men proud of our long tradition of women who are prettier, more decent, and less hairy than European women.

MEDIA WILL BE ORDERLY. Sound, decent science has proven that chaos breeds indecency. Different points of view, while allowed in the Homeland, can foment confusion and mistrust. News will be vetted and spun not once, not twice, but three times by decent editors, publishers, their corporate owners, DOHD, and select religious leaders. It will be read on the air by pretty blond women and virile men, or disseminated by columnists who are not influenced by activist publishers.

WHY YOU WILL BE DECENT

To ensure these goals are achieved in an orderly fashion, the UDA has teeth: It will be enforced by the **LookSee**. DOHD agents will be patrolling neighborhoods and cities in great big black SUVs, fully loaded with the most current high-tech devices: binoculars, X-ray machines, and onboard computers with worldwide databases. They are allowed to enter any building or vehicle, even if you do not occupy it at the time.[3]

In addition, high-tech snooping equipment is listening to billions of phone calls every day, seeking any of the keywords of indecency. We can't tell you what these keywords are, but when our equipment hears them, they go into red alert and flag anyone using these words for further investigation.

---

[3] Agents will soon have the keys to everything in the Homeland.

Do not fear this. Think of the LookSee as your friend. And be reassured by the DOHD motto:

> You have nothing to fear
> if you have nothing to hide.
>
> You have nothing to hide
> if you have nothing to fear.
>
> So fear nothing
> and you need not hide.
>
> Hide nothing
> and you need not fear.[4]

[4]Versions of our motto embroidered by shut-ins and suitable for framing are available for $25 from DOHD. Five dollars of the price goes to help the shut-ins get out more. It is a tax-deductible gift if you make over $300,000 a year.

> In a decent Homeland family,
> the Mommy and Daddy are never
> dumber than their children.
> —ANONYMOUS

DECENCY BEGINS IN THE HOME

Sound scientists who consult for DOHD have proven that it is just a short journey from an indecent, unkempt home to teen pregnancies, abortions, terrorists lurking in our shopping malls, atheists and liberals working hard to destroy Christmas, activist judges allowing OHFs to get married, and the end of life in the Homeland as we know it.

To stop this, Homeland families must now meet certain Home and Yard Guidelines. These are simple to adapt to anyone's life. Those who have trouble—say, removing dandelions from their yards—will find that in the new, improved (i.e., decent) Homeland, their neighbors will not tolerate it and will report these indecencies to us. This can be avoided by learning the major Home and Yard Guidelines for Decency and following them to the letter.

ARTICLE I: DECENCY TRUMPS PRIVACY
(OR, YOUR HOUSE IS OUR HOUSE)

The Heart of the Homeland is the home. Nowhere else is the need for decency in all things more crucial. Indeed, our march backwards to the future begins in the home.

While DOHD believes a man's home is his castle, decency trumps privacy in all matters of the Homeland.[5] DOHD has the keys to every castle, including yours.

ARTICLE II: A PERFECT HOMELAND FAMILY

In the home, Mommy and Daddy, along with their children, maintain a loving relationship that is based on hard work, discipline, and knowing one's place in the Homeland's grand and glorious scheme for decency. Daddy works hard and provides for the family.

Mommy also works very hard, but in the home. It is her responsibility to wash, dust, mop, disinfect, pick up, hang up, create order and sterility throughout the home, and get pregnant often. She shops and cooks and has dinner on the table for Daddy when he returns home. She submits to her husband in the acceptable Homeland Way. (For specifics, see Section II, Article II: Doing "It" the Homeland Way.)

---

[5]Privacy, a quaint idea first articulated by secular humanists and hedonists, is little more than a blanket thrown over indecency in an attempt to hide it.

The children are quiet, disciplined, and maintain a healthy fear of their parents.[6] If the children are homeschooled by Mommy, they remain in the home until after school and home-work is completed. After that, boys may go outside and engage in decent and wholesome war games. Little girls should remain indoors and play with dolls.

ARTICLE III: PROPER NUTRITION
BEGINS AT HOME

Nutrition is Mommy's responsibility, so she must familiarize herself with what a growing family needs. Our great Homeland food industry is working hard to feed the Homeland with ever-more-nutritious, genetically modified meals enhanced with salt and sugar for great taste and preservatives to make them last.

RED MEAT. Meat nurtured the pioneers in the Old West. Home-landers should honor this history by eating even more meat than the pioneers ever dreamed possible. Homeland meat is safe and good for us and the economy. Families that don't eat meat become weak and pale and unable to defend their country against the forces of indecency, which are often non-meat-eating terrorists.

Vegetarianism is unacceptable in the Homeland. It places the Homeland at terrible risk.

---

[6]And for good reason. Corporal punishment, when administered by a loving man, pre-pares children for their future.

ORGANIC FOODS. Organic products tend to be expensive, small, bruised, sugar-free, and produced or manufactured without the aid of our Homeland fertilizer/insecticide/herbicide corporations. The Mommy who buys fresh fruits and vegetables exclusively is not taking advantage of the frozen and processed foods that Homeland manufacturers strive so hard to make uniform and attractive. Additionally, fresh organic food does not have a long shelf life and is therefore of no use to Homeland families during crises (e.g., blizzards, terrorist attacks on traditional marriage, activist judges' decisions).

THE REFRIGERATOR. What you put on the outside of your refrigerator says as much about you as the inside. Grocery lists are wholesome. *Doonesbury* comic strips are not.

ARTICLE IV: A PERFECT EXTERIOR

Weeds signify a lack of discipline and personal responsibility. DOHD strives for a chemical service sign on every lawn to show that homeowners care about liberating the Homeland of dandelions, crabgrass, creeping Jenny and Charlie, or clover. Weeds are often used by the indecent to cover up anything in the yard that might be smokable, psychedelic, or mind-altering.

The lawn should be mowed in an easy-to-understand back-and-forth pattern. Artistic willy-nilly mowing is not easy to understand and is often a coded message to other members of hidden sleeper cells of the indecent.

Gardens should not spill over onto lawns. There must be a

clear line between the two, just as there is a clear line between decency and indecency. Wildflowers or anything termed "native" is not an acceptable substitute for grass.[7]

Shrubbery must be modest and not take up more space than the lawn. There should always be more lawn than shrubbery, gardens, and garden ornaments. When planting any new yard, please refer to the DOHD "Manual on Lawns" for lawn-to-shrubbery-to-garden-to-lawn ornament ratios.

Those who wish to ornament their yards may do so, but not in a way that draws undue attention. Gnomes, wishing wells with elves, crèches or mangers (any time of the year), jockeys, deer, the Homeland's flag, or wooden cutouts of the backside of an elderly woman bending over her garden are all acceptable.

A UN flag, lawn signs protesting any Homeland policy or practice, and peace signs are not. A yard cluttered[8] with peace signs or the UN flag interferes with your neighbor's right to decency.

ARTICLE V: THE HOME LOOKSEE

Agents will make random checks of every Homeland citizen's home. You may assist the DOHD agents by always keeping your drapes open. Closed drapes raise suspicion. When you see the big black DOHD SUVs in your neighborhood, turn on your

---

[7]Bluegrasses and perennial ryes are good examples of decent grasses. DOHD is also very excited about genetically modified grasses that always look very green, neat, and freshly mown and are genetically engineered to survive excessive herbicide use to keep out weeds.

[8]"Cluttered" is hereby defined as one or more of any unacceptable item.

lights both outside and inside. Call someone on the phone as well, so agents can listen in. This will make it easier for DOHD agents to know what's going on in your home.

In cases where DOHD agents need to do more than just look, they will knock on your door for a more in-depth LookSee. If you are not at home, they will let themselves in with their Homeland Key.

The following is a partial listing of what a DOHD agent will look at during the typical Home LookSee. It is impossible for us to provide a complete list because new items are being added all the time, whenever we feel like it, for reasons we can't talk about because it will tip off the indecent.

OUTSIDE THE HOME

CARS. DOHD likes to see two cars parked neatly in the driveway or in the garage. They should be at least midsize sedans and preferably station wagons, vans, or SUVs. Cars must not be rusty, dented, or otherwise old. DOHD likes new cars. New cars show that you support your neighbors and the Homeland by spending money to support the Homeland auto industry.

HOUSING MATERIALS. Housing materials are left to the owner's discretion. However, solar panels indicate you are thumbing your nose at the Homeland's energy industry. This industry works tirelessly to keep the Homeland healthy and strong, and if Homelanders don't support it, it will need tax breaks and even more government support and contracts to remain robust.

INSIDE THE HOME

READING MATERIALS. What kinds of magazines are on your coffee table? Is it the *Utne Reader* (indecent) or *The National Review* (decent)? Which newspapers? Which books? Are they by Al Franken or Jon Stewart (both very indecent)? Or a Harlequin romance and the Bible (good, decent, and wholesome)? Are there books of essays on your coffee table? DOHD is opposed to essays.[9]

WHERE DO YOU SURF? The websites of French newspapers? Have you ever visited Michael Moore's website, even accidentally?

YOUR ANSWERING MACHINE. It will help us if you keep a list of incoming and outgoing calls, along with subject matter, length of call, and how much you like the person you talked to, just in case we were too busy to listen in. This is very important to know, in case we determine the person you called to be indecent. In that case, we might need to investigate you, your family, your

[9]Essays are always about things like growing up homeless, pollution in national parks, or government corruption, subjects that can turn decent people into indecent radicals in desperation. If you feel you need to know something about these or other subjects, seek out decent journalists listed on the DOHD nonactivist journalist list, available from DOHD for only $5 (plus $10 shipping and handling). These journalists have written many news features on many topics citing DOHD-approved sources.

neighbors, your coworkers, your auto mechanic, your account-
ant, and your dentist further.

YOUR FAMILY ALBUMS. Do you have photos you would not feel
comfortable showing to everyone? Have you ever appeared
naked in a photo? Or on a webcam? Questionable photos will be
confiscated.[10] We will also monitor the number of photos of
your family in normal Homeland situations, such as playing
baseball, eating apple pie, saluting the flag, and praying.

YOUR TELEVISION. What's on TV when we walk in the door? Are
you following the DOHD Viewing Pyramid?[11] Is Fox News its
base? Liberal news programs and sitcoms confuse children and
adults and can turn a whole family into secular humanists who
sleep in on Sunday mornings and miss church.

If you pass your Home LookSee, or any other LookSee mentioned in this manual, the Homeland is becoming more decent
every day because of your efforts.

If you did not pass any of the LookSees, refer to "Appendix A:
Proscribed Punishments" for an explanation of what might
happen to you, your family, and everyone you know.

---

[10]No one will ever see them again, unless they are used to train DOHD agents to maintain their poise and dignity even when confronting the grossest indecencies.
[11]See Section V, Article III to learn what the ideal TV Viewing Pyramid is.

ASK YOURSELF THIS!

Will DOHD find library books in your house? Librarians tend to obstruct and interfere with decency by buying books about indecent subjects written by those who live indecent lifestyles, and that makes libraries very dangerous places for children. Especially the Reference Department, where a child can be exposed to "it," experimental theater, and vegetarianism.[12] **Ask yourself this:** What could my children learn at the library that I don't know and that would make me feel stupid if I didn't know it before they did?[13] Why wouldn't I rather have my children do research at home, where parental locks have been placed on the Internet and on the television?

[12]Vegetarians are suspect because they prevent our meat industry from prospering. They are behind the mad cow hysteria. They prevent their children from producing and maintaining the red blood cells and big muscles that can be achieved only by eating more meat than anyone else in the world. Is there a vegetarian in your house? **If so, ask yourself these questions:** Who would be more likely to protect you from terrorists—a meat-and-potatoes man, or a garbanzo bean-loaf man? Which would have the strength in his fingers to defuse a terrorist bomb—the soldier who snacks on rump roast or the soldier who snacks on trail mix?

[13]In a decent Homeland, the Mommy and Daddy are never dumber than their children.

DOHD scientists have proven that
Mommies who try to initiate "it" make
men nervous and anxious and unsure
of the masculinity that is so crucial in
maintaining our Homeland's potency,
firmness, and decency.

How to Do "It"[14]
in a Decent Home

ARTICLE I: TALKING ABOUT "IT"

How we in the Homeland handle "it"—whether talking about "it," thinking about "it," teaching about "it," depicting "it" in books and movies, or actually doing "it"—says a lot about us and our proud march backwards to the future. Therefore, when discussing "it," DOHD regulations require everyone to use the term "it" and nothing else. Furthermore, when discussing those private parts used during the actual doing of "it," the only DOHD-approved terms are: "down there," "private parts," "Mr. Johnson," "Mrs. Johnson," "hoo hoo," and "it."

---

[14]It is too indecent to discuss what "it" actually is, but we know you know what we are talking about. We at the Department of Homeland Decency think this is the best way to deal with this mature subject matter.

Only the extreme sensitivity and modesty of this rule will protect everyone in the Homeland from liberals, secular humanists, Hollywood, France, and, of course, homosexual recruitment. This regulation will especially protect our children, who are weak and easily influenced by the aforementioned hedonists, terrorists, and liars.

Discussing "it" in public is immoral. Therefore, it is illegal to discuss "it" unless all the following conditions are met: You are married, are attempting to do "it" with your spouse, are having some kind of problem, and the lights are out; or you are explaining to your children why they don't have to know what "it" is until they are married.

ARTICLE II: DOING "IT" THE HOMELAND WAY

Because our Intelligent Designer designed "it" to be done by a Mommy and a Daddy, the very intimate and private parts of the Mommy and Daddy[15] fit together perfectly when they do "it." This is why they can finish "it" quickly and quietly without moaning or screaming and then get up and go about daily life as if nothing happened.

On the other hand, if two Mommies do it together, or two Daddies, the parts don't fit, causing great pain and anguish, which leads to moaning and screaming, bed-squeaking, joint problems, falling property values, urban blight, STDs, cancer, and vulnerability to terrorist attacks.

---

[15]E.g., Mr. and Mrs. Johnson.

Anyone married can legally do "it" with their spouse if they do "it" the Homeland Way, a method developed by a DOHD panel of male scientists. The Homeland Way is: one man, one woman, in the dark, shades down, doors closed, no protection, no marital aids, no cameras, man on top, woman on bottom, face-to-face, eyes shut, private parts inserted where they are supposed to be and nowhere else, and no fantasizing about liberal Hollywood celebrities while in the act of doing "it." If your mind wanders while you are doing "it," it is acceptable to keep it on topics like sports and hunting (if you are the Daddy) or on ironing (if you are the Mommy).

KEEP IT QUIET. People doing "it" the Homeland Way are very quiet. Your neighbors do not want to know if or when you are doing "it," and neither do their children.

MOMMY IS SUBMISSIVE. In the Homeland Way, initiating "it" is the Daddy's job. Mommies who try to initiate "it" make men nervous and anxious and unsure of the masculinity that is so crucial in maintaining our Homeland's potency, firmness, and decency. Additionally, anxious Daddies married to aggressive Mommies are more likely to drink too much, leaving Mommies thinking bad thoughts about their spouses and men in general. Then they seek "it" outside of marriage with other Mommies, leading to indecent Mommy-Mommy households.

ARTICLE III: DON'T THINK ABOUT "IT"

Thinking about "it" (except in the confines of marriage, and only minutes before doing "it") can slow down our march backwards to the future. Random "it" thoughts make a person dizzy, weak, and sometimes too confused to remain alert to those outside the Homeland who wish to bring their indecencies here. DOHD scientists have shown that those whose minds wander are helped a great deal if they work a second job or do volunteer work for faith-based groups helping shut-ins, where no one has such thoughts.

ARTICLE IV: HOW TO DEPICT "IT" IN BOOKS, MAGAZINES, MOVIES, AND TELEVISION

The only moral way to depict anyone doing "it" outside of marriage in books, magazines,[16] movies, or TV programs is to show them suffering a horrible fate directly caused by doing "it" without the benefit of marriage. The Creative Team of the DOHD Family Viewing Hour Division (see Section V, Article II) has approved a number of fates that must befall characters who do "it" out of wedlock. These fates include: death in a fiery car crash,

---

[16]Magazine "it" quizzes (e.g., "Fifteen Ways to Tell You Are a Great Lover!" or "Forty-seven Tricks to Do with Condoms!") are written by people who are doing "it" all the time, in every indecent place and position, with multicolored condoms and without the sanction of marriage. (For specific questions about media and "it," consult Section V and the Basic Viewing Pyramid as well as Appendix D on the need to turn Hollywood into HOLYwood.)

death in an exploding building, death in a tornado, dismember-
ment of any extremity or limb by any means, being lost at sea,
falling off a roller coaster, maiming, turning homosexual, getting
a horrible disease that includes all-over body boils, especially on
Mr. and Mrs. Johnson, or being the cause of another 9/11.

In addition, teens doing "it" can suffer the following fates:
Cheerleaders will develop chronic acne and lose their cheerlead-
ing positions; athletes will suffer horrible injuries because they
are thinking about doing "it" and not thinking about the big
game when the ball hits them hard in the head and puts them in
a coma for years; honor students will become addicted to drugs
or gambling and end up destitute and homeless; computer
geniuses will seek easy riches by hacking into the computers of
Homeland corporations and end up suffering horribly in prison
by playing Mommy to some other prisoner's Daddy.

ARTICLE V: ZERO TOLERANCE

Any Homelander who is aware that their children or a friend's,
neighbor's, or stranger's children are being urged to learn about
and carry condoms on their person is duty-bound to talk them
out of learning about or carrying those items. They will try to
sweet-talk you with unsound facts about preventing disease
or death, but you must tell them that learning about and carrying contraceptives is tantamount to doing "it" every day with
everyone and having many abortions, which will make them
nonmarriage material. If you have trouble convincing these
young people of these science-based facts, DOHD can supply

you with lots of realistic drawings and pictures of aborted fetuses that will be helpful in your conversations. Be sure to remind them that a healthy Homeland is filled with married people who have lots of children and have never had abortions.

ARTICLE VI: TEACHING "IT"

DOHD supports and now enforces abstinence-only education—at school AND at home. Using sound science, a DOHD panel of male scientists has proven that you can't do what you know nothing about.

Furthermore, DOHD is formulating a new policy that goes beyond abstinence education and promises to provide total protection for our children and the Homeland: "Abstaining from Abstinence Discussions." The most effective abstinence education of all, this will put "it" back where it belongs—in the marriage bed, in the dark, under lots of blankets.

But until that happens, abstinence-only education in the home must follow a specific format. If your child asks you anything about "it," you must use the following format to answer the questions:

Your Child: Mommy, where do babies come from?

You: From married Mommies and Daddies.

Your Child: How does it happen?

You: Married Mommies and Daddies do "it" when they want to have a baby.

Your Child: Will I do "it," too?

You: Yes, when you are married and not before. If you do "it"
before, you will die or get a disfiguring rash or you will cause
another 9/11.

After "Abstaining from Abstinence Discussions" is law in the
Homeland, the format for discussing "it" with your child will
change, as follows:

Your Child: Mommy, where do babies come from?
You: Go clean your room.

ARTICLE VII: THE "IT" LOOKSEE

Agents will make random checks of every Homeland home and
school for indications of "it" being talked about, thought about,
depicted, taught, or done outside of DOHD rules. The following
are some of what our agents look for. Some merely raise an eye-
brow. Some, combined with others, cause great concern. Some,
all by themselves, nauseate even our most hardened agents.

FANCY BATHS, HOT TUBS, AND SAUNAS. Do you own a hot tub,
whirlpool, or sauna? Does your shower have see-through curtains or no curtains at all? Are you doing something more than
taking a bath or shower? Secular humanists answer "Yes" to all
these questions. They use these items for something other than
cleanliness or therapy: for hedonistic pleasures. As a result, many
young, attractive, naive Homeland women are lured into situations where they end up doing "it" in their bathing suits.

FANCY UNDERWEAR. Avoid fancy underwear, silk underwear, and especially underwear with indecent wording around Mr. or Mrs. Johnson (like "Enter Here" or "Man at Work").

GYM MEMBERSHIPS. Many Homelanders spend too much time at the gym sweating, trying to become a "hottie." Exercising with others in skimpy outfits always leads to doing "it" in unapproved locations (e.g., in swimming pools, on Nautilus machines, on trampolines).

CLOSETS. Do you have a friend or family member in the closet? We don't mind, as long as they stay there.

CONDOMS. We look everywhere for condoms. We ask your pharmacists, too. And your trash haulers. They like to talk about these things.

UNUSUAL FOODS. Food is a precursor to doing "it," so our agents seek out those foods most likely to lead to recreational "it."[17] If there are more than three of these in your home, or even just one in your bedroom, you are hopelessly tainted and do "it" recreationally.

ASK YOURSELF THIS!

Visit your children's school. If their biology classroom displays anatomical charts of the human body, know that it is a pretense

[17]These include but are not limited to: chocolates, French wines, stinky cheeses, baguettes, oysters, lobster, plates of fresh fruit, peeled grapes, figs, French-roasted coffee beans, espresso, extra-virgin olive oil, and Paul Newman products.

for teaching "it." If their art class teacher tells them the human form is beautiful, it is a pretense for teaching "it." The school is no place for discussions of "it." It confuses and embarrasses children and, in turn, confuses and embarrasses their parents when the children seem to know more about "it" than they do. Additionally, teaching children to put condoms on cucumbers, zucchini, carrots, rutabagas, and potatoes gives them the wrong idea about what vegetables are for. **Ask yourself this:** Would you rather your child learn that vegetables are to be boiled and placed next to a large piece of meat on the dinner plate, or that vegetables can take the place of a "hoo hoo"?

While DOHD frowns on marital aids, it understands that Mr. Johnson occasionally needs outside help. This is normal. Fortunately, the Homeland's pharmaceutical industry has answered this cry for help. The problem occurs when men want to make their women pregnant, contented, and fulfilled by doing "it," but Mr. Johnson takes a nap. When this happens, DOHD supports the use of Viagra and all the other similar drugs as advertised on TV, but no other marital aids. **Ask yourself this:** Do decent corporations spend lots of money to develop faulty products? Will a contented Mommy stay home and make the neighborhood more decent? How many little decent citizens are the direct result of Viagra and other similar pharmaceutical breakthroughs? What could be more patriotic than supporting the Homeland's pharmaceutical giants?

Nothing says "Homeland"
better than a sandwich.

DECENCY IN THE WORKPLACE

If the Home is the Heart of the Homeland, then the Workplace is its Kidneys. It is in the workplace where the enormous work of the Homeland is accomplished. In the workplace, men (and sometimes women who are childless or women who have children and are selfish) practice the true character of the Homeland. When their decency is firm and potent, this creates a strong united front for decency for the whole world to see.

The workplace molds or replaces, produces or throws out, hires or fires, promotes or demotes. In essence, it cleanses the Homeland of impurities by purging those who do not contribute to our march backwards to the future.

The flushing of indecency—the bile of the Homeland—is best accomplished with healthy kidneys. If there is too much poison in the system, one kidney may fail and the work must be done by just one. An overabundance of indecency may cause total kidney failure. At that point, the workplace—indeed, possibly the whole Homeland—must be put on dialysis.

ARTICLE I: PROPER DRESS

While it is natural and even desirable for men to harbor indecent thoughts,[18] these thoughts are doubly intense when women dress provocatively at work, especially on Casual Fridays. Flaunting of femininity creates cracks in men's morale and leads to what liberals call sexual harassment, but which DOHD social scientists now know is really nothing more than demoralized, emasculated men trying to regain their rightful spots in the hierarchy of the workplace by giving in to their natural instinct to mate with women who wear short skirts or tight blue jeans on Fridays.

Women in the workplace must now wear clothing approved by DOHD-contracted fashion designers.[19] Casual Fridays and the clothing once associated with that day are now banned.

ARTICLE II: SEXUAL HARASSMENT IS BANNED

The best solution to sexual harassment (or demoralized, emasculated men trying to regain their rightful spots) in the work-

---

[18]These are the very thoughts and urges that keep the Homeland well populated with decent people. Decent men fight these urges 24/7, a struggle our Intelligent Designer intended. By struggling and eventually conquering lust and indecent thoughts, a decent man becomes very strong and very wise.

[19]Cardigans, midcalf skirts, panty hose, low pumps, plain makeup.

place is not to report it. Court cases are long and complex because one side usually lies in these cases. Those who charge their bosses with sexual harassment end up tired, defeated, and bitter, which taints the workplace and hurts morale and productivity.

Because bosses talk with bosses in other Homeland corporations, this can also get the spouses of those filing discrimination lawsuits fired from their jobs in other workplaces and make them unable to find work ever again.

ARTICLE III: MEN SHOULD NOT WORK FOR WOMEN

Many men now work for women. DOHD scientists have studied these men and found that they almost always end up divorced, because their wives do not respect men who work for women. Women are often promoted ahead of more qualified men because of liberal workplace quotas that place a person's gender above a person's abilities.

This ignores the finely honed leadership abilities of men that have been passed down from one generation of men to the next because of their constant struggle with lust and indecent thoughts (see footnote 18). Therefore, when companies are considering whom to hire or promote, being a man must carry extra weight in making personnel decisions.

ARTICLE IV: WOMEN, CHILDREN, AND DAY CARE

Because so many women now work, children are left home alone or put in day care centers. Children left to their own devices at home watch television. These children often watch *Teletubbies* (and other European psychedelic drug-induced programming whose characters are often gay) or *Sesame Street,* whose puppets support the politics of diversity.

In addition, these same children may be under the control of day care providers who ban toy guns from the premises, teach them games that do not promote the concept of winning at all costs, and don't practice corporal punishment. These are the very things that will make our children strong enough to survive if they are captured by terrorists and tortured.

ARTICLE V: DECENCY IN THE LUNCHROOM

Multiculturism and Diversity are diseases masquerading as opportunity. Both concepts originate from liberal freethinkers and other enemies of the Homeland.

When these concepts meet the reality of the Homeland Workplace, there is much confusion, which often results in bitterness. Women and other kinds of people of color, religion, and handicap are given jobs that many of our Homeland white men deserve just as much. Suddenly, the workplace is filled with languages other than English, including Black, Spanish, Indian, and the like. The workplace lunchroom is no longer a restful spot to consume a hamburger or doughnut; instead, foods like hummus and salsa take up space in the company refrigerator.

Finally, workers become exposed to foreign work concepts that may corrupt decent work habits: long lunch breaks where fancy foreign food is served, lingering over lunches, drinking wine with lunch, and so on.

While DOHD applauds a melting-pot society, what happens when the soup is full of lumps? Therefore, workplace lunch-rooms must always serve Homeland cuisine, and those who bring their lunch should remember that nothing says "Homeland" better than a sandwich.

ARTICLE VI: THE WORKPLACE LOOKSEE

DOHD agents will make frequent checks of every Homeland business. To ensure proper compliance to DOHD rules, all checks will be surprise checks. While DOHD understands that this frightens some companies, many Homeland employees are right now "in flagrante delicto."[20] If all bosses and employees study what DOHD is looking for, there is no need to worry about fines and/or punishments. Remember: DOHD is like a giant dialysis machine that purifies the body of the Homeland by purging the workplace[21] of all poisons.

The following are some—but not all—criteria that will help your company complete a successful LookSee. We cannot

---

[20]E.g., a worker refusing to join a prayer team; a worker riding his bicycle to work when his SUV is in perfect running condition.

[21]I.e., the kidneys.

provide all the criteria, because that would provide a road map for the indecent to infiltrate corporate boardrooms everywhere.

Outward Appearance

CONSERVATIVE DRESS. DOHD likes to see well-dressed, smiling employees who look busy. Dress should be conservative, clean, and modest. If the boss is a woman, she should be dressed like a woman. Female bosses who dress in pants confuse their male underlings about their own sexuality and can also give rise to urges that belong only in pornographic films.

NOT TOO FASHIONABLE. Men should try to look like men. While DOHD recognizes that OHFs work among us, special attention will be paid to those who are too "neat," too "scrubbed," or too "fashionable."

NO HEAD COVERINGS. Religious head coverings are acceptable outside the workplace, but not inside. Some head coverings are roomy enough to hide something in. If there is room for a stapler, then there is room for a grenade.

Company Amenities—Use and Overuse

BATHROOM BREAKS. DOHD expects urination breaks in the decent workplace, but overusing this privilege decreases efficiency and tends to make coworkers wonder why you need to urinate so often. DOHD can be expected to do random surprise checks of all bathroom stalls to make sure nothing indecent is being practiced. Lingering during a bathroom break is frowned on. DOHD researchers determined that bathroom breaks should last no more than 41.8 seconds.

LUNCH. DOHD expects lunch breaks to comform to decent workplace standards. What is being eaten? DOHD likes to see luncheon meats, Cheez Whiz, and other foods rich in the Homeland culinary heritage. DOHD makes special note of those eating rice and beans, salads with goat cheese, and cold soups like gazpacho. The length of a decent lunch break is thirty minutes or less. Longer lunch breaks result in less productivity and a greater possibility of engaging in stomach-churning lunchroom conversations about politics, war, and religion, or even doing "it" with some young coworker in a broom closet and thus being too tired to be a highly productive worker the rest of the day.

Company Prayer

PRAYER ZONES. DOHD likes to see company prayer groups and a designated Prayer Zone (see Section VI: Prayer, Intelligent Design, Decency, and You, Articles I and III for regulations on Prayer Zones) that is properly equipped for these groups. DOHD makes special note of those who go to the prayer room as often as they urinate. This is suspicious and makes DOHD believe you are neither urinating nor praying when you say you are.

Office Supplies

EMPLOYEE THEFT. Office supplies belong in the office, not in the home. DOHD expects each company boss to appoint someone who will inform DOHD about who is taking how many staplers and pencils and how long it has been going on. DOHD realizes that this type of thievery is rampant in all Homeland workplaces, and although it cannot imprison you or cut off your hands the way they do in other countries, DOHD is able to impose stiff penalties and administer other unpleasant stuff.

Salary, Vacations, and Medical Benefits

BE BUSINESS SMART. DOHD cannot set salary guidelines, award raises, or set vacation and medical benefit policies for companies. But it believes that a spoiled worker is a soft worker. A soft worker is one more likely to be well rested and self-satisfied, and thus more prone to be thinking of ways to make themselves happy, which makes it easy for any indecent terrorist to walk right in and sit down in that person's cubicle without that worker even noticing.

ASK YOURSELF THIS!

There are many problems associated with women bosses. The key for workers is to make sure they understand the special problems women have. **If your boss is a woman, ask yourself this:** What should you remember when "her aunt comes to visit"? How about when she has a "bun in the oven"? How you answer can mean the difference between merit increase and demotion.

Men are playful bosses. They relieve tensions through playing and joking, especially with their female workers. This can lead to misunderstandings. **If your boss is a man, ask yourself this:** What should you remember when he is "just kidding around" or when he tells you to "relax" or "lighten up"? What you decide can mean the difference between a large raise and being fired.

If the person in the next cubicle is a foreigner, do you share the Homeland culture's products and heritage with them in order to help them help the Homeland become stronger and more decent? **Ask yourself this:** If you are eating a Big Mac and they are eating fried rice, should you offer them a bite of your burger? If that person is wearing a big scarf over their head and mouth, do you show them your ski cap with the ball on top and show how you hang it in the closet when you get to work? Do you offer to let them try it on? Sharing your culture can mean changing minds and stopping another 9/11 at work and at home.

How are your kidneys functioning? Literally and figuratively? Remember: The clogged kidneys of the workplace can break the heart of the home.

Death fosters decency by building character. Sick folks who smoke pot to avoid some of the negative aspects of death are sending the wrong message to young Homelanders. They are saying that it is OK to use drugs when things get tough.

[SECTION IV]

Medical Decency

ARTICLE I: THE FEEDING TUBE

In the Age of Decency, the feeding tube will be a badge of honor. It says that you and your loved ones respect life, that you will not allow secular humanists, scientists, doctors, or other New Age types let you pass on before you are actually called to your eternal reward by our Intelligent Designer.[22]

To make sure that everyone who needs a feeding tube gets one—and won't have it yanked out—the **Neighborhood Decency Posse (NDP)** (see Appendix B) will assist in the

---

[22]DOHD sells tie clips, earrings, and small pins in the shape of feeding tubes so decent Homelanders can show their support for a culture of life. Made by shut-ins, they are $75 each ($5 of each pin goes to shut-ins) and make wonderful holiday and birthday gifts. It is a tax-deductible purchase if you make over $300,000 per year.

placement of feeding tubes[23] as well as in the removal of feeding tubes when and only when the Homelander recovers or dies. The Posse Members will be armed during these critical moments.

To help make these important decisions, the Neighborhood Decency Posse will consult with physicians, loved ones, health insurance companies, Fox News, concerned evangelical organizations, William Bennett, Ann Coulter, and DOHD and then shall issue a report on why the feeding tube was or was not inserted.

Because the Neighborhood Decency Posses are our front line against indecency, their many other duties may delay such a report. If they are staking out an indecent home or business in their neighborhood, that must be their priority. In those cases, the feeding tube must be put in and remain in until the Neighborhood Decency Posse roots out that indecency and gets around to writing a report on the feeding tube.

ARTICLE II: HOW TO PREVENT INSERTION

DOHD recognizes that there will be some situations where Homelanders will not want a feeding tube inserted. In these cases, they must fill out a living will in triplicate and send it to DOHD. They must also include a detailed essay explaining

---

[23]DOHD polled twenty-eight adults sitting in the front three rows of a Pat Robertson revival and asked the following question: Would you: (a) want a doctor on his way to buy a new Porsche to examine you and say you were brain dead; or (b) have your Neighborhood Decency Posse examine you and say you have plenty of productive years left? Over 97 percent of them, representing 275 million Homelanders (with a margin of error of plus or minus 65 percent), chose (b). They also said they think doctors play too much golf, drive cars that are too fancy, eat everything they tell their patients not to eat, and would rather make money off an abortion warehouse than practice decent medicine.

why they are opposed to the Homeland's culture of life and list how their parents, grandparents, siblings, aunts, uncles, and cousins died and whether they would approve of this decision, why they would or would not approve, and how they can be sure that is what they would be thinking. They then must take a drug test to make sure they aren't making a decision based on drug addiction rather than heartfelt logic, reasoning, and spiritual understanding. Their minister[24] must vouch for their character in a two-thousand-word[25] essay. And they must also locate a high school teacher who knew them well and who can state that they were of upstanding character in high school.

Patients who want a feeding tube do not need to do anything.

ARTICLE III: FROZEN EMBRYOS

Because embryos are living human beings who are among the most vulnerable Homelanders among us, we must refer to them more respectfully. Therefore, frozen embryos will be called "homeless embryos."

ARTICLE IV: HOMELESS EMBRYOS

A decent Homeland will not create homeless embryos in order to destroy them and then take their stem cells.

---

[24]If they do not have a minister, DOHD will appoint one for them, who will interview them to determine their ability to make this decision decently.

[25]This means it must be between 1,975 and 2,025 words. Anything outside those parameters is unacceptable.

A decent Homeland will find a home for all its homeless citizens, even the smallest and most vulnerable ones. Therefore, it is DOHD's official policy to find all homeless embryos and their stem cells a home. For too long they have been kept in refrigerators and freezers and ignored throughout the Homeland because unsound science said that time stopped for them as long as they remained frozen. DOHD scientists have proven that time continues to pass for homeless embryos and stem cells, and research shows that, with the passage of time, they are increasingly eager to find a home.

Therefore, DOHD orders all childless couples to come forward and be implanted with a homeless embryo so that said embryo and its stem cells can have a good home.

DOHD orders everyone, even liberals and secular humanists, to support this initiative. Those who don't can be sued for nonsupport by homeless embryos once they have grown up.

ARTICLE V: MEDICAL MARIJUANA

DOHD believes that death fosters decency by building character. Those who smoke pot to avoid some of the negative aspects of death are sending the wrong message to young Homelanders. They are saying that it is OK to use drugs when things get tough.

DOHD is opposed to this practice because once the person's pain is relieved by this practice, they feel good enough to use other drugs to feel even better. They then end up addicted for the remainder of their lives to cocaine, heroin, meth, or OxyContin, and there is nothing sadder than a sick person confined to bed trying to inject an illegal drug when the nurses aren't looking. DOHD works closely with the DEA and can arrange for a quick search, seizure, and arrest of the offending patient—at home, in the hospital, or in a nursing home. DOHD believes that a strong Homeland is made up of people strong enough to withstand any kind of pain or suffering. We confront difficulties head-on, become more decent through them, and pass on our experiences to others.

Therefore, medical marijuana is banned.

ARTICLE VI: THE MORNING-AFTER PILL

The name of this pill suggests that something happened the night before that is very significant—significant enough to have a pill named after it. Something that significant should not be erased.

Therefore, the morning-after pill cannot be purchased anywhere in the Homeland. DOHD does not have jurisdiction over Canada or other Third World countries, but it is devising a profile of likely users of this drug. Airport security around the nation has been alerted and will profile those flying to Canada or other Third World countries. Those fitting the profile will be delayed for up to two days, thus making this pill useless for them.

ARTICLE VII: THE DOCTOR-RELIGION RELATIONSHIP

Patients may ask their physicians what church they attend, and if they do not like the answer, they do not have to pay any doctor's fees.

ARTICLE VIII: THE MEDICAL LOOKSEE

All medical charts will be deposited in a central location.

When checking out medical decency in the Homeland, DOHD agents will select charts at random for review. To help DOHD agents remain efficient, DOHD orders all physicians to write clearly and use only simple words. It would be best if all abbreviations, jargon, and difficult scientific terms were explained in detail at the beginning of the chart or not used at all.

The following are the important questions DOHD agents will try to answer in their random physician interviews:

Does the physician love children and want all his women patients to have lots of children? Will he[26] do everything he can to make sure she has lots of kids and obeys her husband? Is the

---

[26]DOHD believes that physicians should be men because of their natural ability to reason and make rational decisions.

physician married? Does he have lots of kids of his own? Does he note in the medical records which women visited an abortion warehouse? Why they did? What happened to them there? Whether anyone went to jail? Does he think biblical passages can help women cure their hormonal imbalances and thus make life easier for the men in their lives? Does he use prayer as a first line of treatment? Does he advocate prayer as preventive medicine? Does he support feminism? Or does he tell his women patients that they can develop cancer if they go braless?

From these ongoing interviews, DOHD will continuously update a Homeland Medical Registry. Anyone looking for a decent physician will then be able to easily find one near their home or workplace.

ASK YOURSELF THIS!

If you support abortion, you could develop cancer. DOHD-sponsored research has found a strong connection between support for abortion and painful, inoperable tumors of the hoo hoo. **Ask yourself this:** Do I want to risk a slow, painful death just so hedonists can have a good time? Do I want to risk a slow, painful death just so I don't have to face the consequences of my actions?

Your ninety-eight-year-old grandfather smokes, drinks, curses, stays up late, listens to rock and roll, and ogles cheerleaders during TV basketball games. You think he has Alzheimer's disease and suggest putting him in a home, but the family thinks it's not necessary because the booze and smoking will kill him soon enough. **Ask yourself this:** If the family places a Do Not Resuscitate order on his medical record and you are there when he has a heart attack, would you resuscitate him? Is he decent enough to be resuscitated? Should only the decent be resuscitated? Do you support a culture of life that includes people like your grandfather?

TV shows must always have a robust respect and awe of the President. He must always be depicted as smart, tall, muscular, and handsome, and preferably shown riding a horse or driving an ATV through rugged terrain, unless, of course, he is a weak-willed Democrat.

DECENCY AND THE FIVE BUILDING BLOCKS OF HEALTHY TV VIEWING

Control TV and you control Homeland decency.

There are those, however, who want us to turn TV off and get to know our neighbors and families better. Not only is that naive, it could be anti-Homeland. What if your neighbors aren't so decent? What if they do "it" in the dining room? How will that affect you?

Creating decent programming avoids that problem. Decent Programming is another tool for strengthening the Homeland. So DOHD, with the approval of the FCC, has made the following changes to the Homeland airwaves. These will ensure decency for years to come as well as make American TV a model for other countries, even those that regularly feature nude newscasters.

ARTICLE I: THE FAMILY VIEWING HOUR

The Family Viewing Hour will be changed from **7 p.m.–9 p.m.** to **5 a.m.–Midnight**. During this time period, only Decent Programming can be shown.

ARTICLE II: DECENT PROGRAMMING

Decent Programming (**DP**) is programming that promotes and encourages Homeland ideas and values (e.g., buy that SUV) and prevents exposure to anti-Homeland ideas and values (e.g., that SUV wastes lots of gas. Buy this modest, inexpensive, foreign car).

Working closely with the FCC, the Creative Team of the DOHD Family Viewing Hour Division has developed guidelines that programs must meet to be rated DP. To make this simpler to understand, the CT-DOHD-FVH Div. has created the five basic building blocks of TV viewing. DOHD scientists have shown that watching a recommended minimum daily amount in each block guarantees decency.[27] These basic blocks are:

1. Dramatic programs about families
2. Sound News shows (especially shows about Young Attractive White Women Who Go Missing)

---

[27]Decent Homelanders can maintain a strong level of decency with just two hours of daily viewing in each group. Indecent Homelanders will require more, but the amount will be determined individually.

3. Programs depicting Celebrity Worship
4. Reality shows
5. Sports

DOHD has established decency guidelines for all programming in each of these basic viewing groups.

Family Dramas Must Have:

ONE DADDY AND ONE MOMMY. A family show may feature one parent only if the other parent is dead or fighting overseas. Divorce or separation can be shown only if it is caused by a home-wrecking, liberal, East or West Coast college professor, or like person. The story line becomes compelling because the homewrecker must then, by order of DOHD, become addicted to drugs and (a) fall off a bridge or in front of a semi while on drugs; (b) die in a house fire while on drugs; (c) step on a rusty nail and get tetanus while on drugs; or (d) be swept away in a flash flood or other disaster while on drugs.[28] The adulterer must also be punished for his or her indecency, either dying with the person they did "it" with or suffering horribly in some other punishing manner.

AT LEAST ONE CHILD, BUT PREFERABLY MORE. If the family does not have children, it must be because the Mommy and Daddy cannot have children because they grew up in the Sixties

---

[28]Any fate not listed here must be approved by the Creative Team of the DOHD Family Viewing Hour Division. It also must clearly be punishment for doing "it" with a married person.

and did illegal drugs that made them sterile. They can try to adopt, but they must be turned down for being former drug addicts. A family show can never present a Mommy and Daddy who make a decision not to have children and are happy about it.

ONE PARENT WORKS OUTSIDE THE HOME. It is preferable that the Daddy work outside the home, unless he is very ill or is recovering from injuries caused by fighting terrorists overseas. In this case, the Mommy can work, but she must explain to her children in each episode that she is doing this because the Daddy is a hero and needs his rest.

NO "IT" TALK IN THE HOME. Pregnancy is permitted in family shows but cannot be discussed. Jokes about pregnancy and how Mommy got pregnant are forbidden. A Mommy may be pregnant during the first half of a program and then be sitting in her kitchen with the new baby after a commercial break. Mommies and Daddies do not discuss "it" with each other or with their children. The viewer must be able to assume from the plot and dialogue that any discussion of "it" was conducted between the parents and the children in private. Children may not give any indications that they know about "it," unless plot elements require them to talk about "it" and/or be punished for doing "it" by failing school, getting a disease, or ending up in jail. DOHD does not require it but would like to see corporal punishment at least once in each episode, meted out either by the Daddy or a teacher.

NEIGHBORS AS SYMBOLIC STEREOTYPES. Neighbors should be used to show the failings of the indecent. Amusing stories about secular humanist/atheist or lesbian neighbors—for example, depicting them as impractical, dumb, ugly, out of shape, funnily dressed, or with the wrong kind of haircut for a girl—will help ensure that Homeland children do not see these kinds of people as role models. Using humor (such as locking OHFs in a coat closet) is highly recommended.

Sound News Shows Are Required to Have:

ROBUST RESPECT AND AWE OF THE PRESIDENT.[29] The President must be depicted as smart, tall, muscular, and handsome. The viewer must be able to imagine him[30] being as comfortable sitting in an armored tank as in the Oval Office.

LOTS OF STORIES OF YOUNG ATTRACTIVE WHITE WOMEN WHO GO MISSING. These stories make all decent Homelanders proud that we still produce more Young Attractive Decent White Women than anywhere else in the world. Women in these stories must be shown reverently; the more virginal they look, the better. If guns are a part of this story, care must taken to show that 99 percent of all Homeland gun owners are decent men who care for and protect the decency and virginity of Young Attractive White Women, especially those who Go Missing.

---

[29]The only exception to this is if the President is a weak-willed Democrat.

[30]Until women learn to control their hormones, DOHD does not support the idea of a woman as President.

SOUND NEWS DELIVERED BY ATTRACTIVE NEWS ANCHORS. Sound news is in the same family as sound science. It means that all news has been vetted for balanced fairness and facts that cannot be spun toward the liberal point of view. Attractive news anchors are those who are able to move their lips. Men should be strong and manly. Women should be blond and womanly.

DECENT SPONSORSHIP. DP news cannot be sponsored by condom or birth-control companies, unless equal time is given during news programming to present sound news stories concerning people doing "it" out of wedlock and suffering disease, death, or both.

Celebrity Worship Must Have:

MINDLESSNESS. It is important for Homeland DP TV to be mindless so viewers can enjoy occasional respites from the serious perils our Homeland faces every day. The more mindless, the more likely it is to get a DP rating. Thus, it is not enough for these shows to tell who is dating whom, who is going on what vacation, who is a good golfer, and which starlet is adopting a baby outside the Homeland. To receive a DP rating, they also must tell us who eats what, who shops where, who suffered a bad sunburn in Mexico, who dislikes being a celebrity, who is depressed and why, and who likes making movies with Tom Cruise . . . and who doesn't.

Reality Shows Are Required to Have:

STRESSFUL REALITY. Plots or situations that teach the Homeland viewer how to handle stressful situations in order to be prepared for the real stresses of daily life. Eating a bowl of spiders, being submerged in mud, being forced to date an unattractive woman—all of these stressful situations, especially when combined with monetary rewards, teach us how to react when real life threatens the Homeland.

Sports Shows Are Required to Have:

YOUNG, BEAUTIFUL, CHEERING WOMEN. These women may be cheerleaders or in the stands. It is important for all cameramen to focus on these women when there is a stoppage of play.

THE HOMELAND ANTHEM, FLAGS, JETS, AND PRAYER. The anthem must precede all sports play. Homeland flags must be raised during the anthem. Jets must fly overhead after flags are raised. Prayer is suggested before play begins.

ACCIDENTS, MINOR INJURIES, AND FIGHTS. DP programming allows for sports violence during the Family Viewing Hour because sports teach that, as in war, defending the goalpost (decency) and winning the game (Homeland) means sacrifice.

FAST CARS. DOHD believes that NASCAR is the best way to incorporate all Homeland values in a single programming time slot. NASCAR races through all Homeland values in one afternoon: crashes, prayers, attractive women, flags, military jets, the anthem, accidents, minor injuries, and death. All NASCAR programming is automatically given DP approval.

ARTICLE III: DP TV VIEWING PYRAMIDS

Viewing habits that reinforce decency are structured in the following pyramids. There is only one ideal DP Viewing Pyramid. It is compact and strong and does not allow any of the major viewing groups to be ignored during the Family Viewing Hour. DOHD scientists have proven that it is the safest way to protect your family and the Homeland from Michael Moore, Jane Fonda, French cooking shows, and the like.

IDEAL VIEWING PYRAMID

The Ideal Viewing Pyramid (Figure A) is based soundly on the Sound News Basic Building Block, with Family and Sports groups adding strength. No amount of Homeland-bashing by Jane Fonda types will cause this pyramid to collapse. This pyramid provides a base of decency that will protect you and your family from all the threats to Homeland decency that are out there.

FIGURE A

PROBLEM PYRAMIDS

Many viewers come close to the ideal pyramid but make basic mistakes, are lazy, or simply don't care that any substitution makes them and the Homeland vulnerable to all kinds of threats.

In Figure B, for instance, a viewer tries to replace some of the

FIGURE B

Sports Group with PBS, which causes him to fall asleep during stories of Young Attractive White Women Gone Missing. PBS stories of aborigines or penguin fertility rites can cause one side of the pyramid to weaken and even collapse. This is like getting the flu. While "under the weather" and weakened, one is very susceptible to further enticements of the indecent.

In Figure C, a viewer makes Cinemax movies, which usually star Young Attractive Shapely Women Who Are Topless, the base of his viewing pyramid instead of the Sound News Group. But because so many of this viewer's coworkers pay attention to the numerous stories about Young Attractive White Girls Gone Missing and talk about them at work, this viewer experiences extreme guilt and confusion. The viewer becomes more isolated, watches more Cinemax movies featuring Young Attractive Shapely Women Who Are Topless, is unable to join regular conversations with coworkers, is fired for being antisocial, and finally turns to drugs for relief.

In Figure D, a viewer replaces the Reality Group with a liberal

FIGURE C

FIGURE D

Faux Reality Group that airs a documentary on medical mari-juana. This type of tinkering is dangerous because it exposes the viewer and his family to anti-Homeland ideas and ideals that lead to the slippery slope of drug experimentation, showing up to work late, getting fired, and then burglarizing homes to support a drug habit.

In Figure E, a viewer decides to watch C-SPAN instead of the

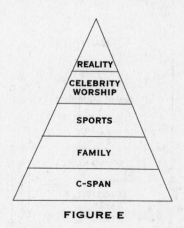

FIGURE E

Sound News programming. This can be more dangerous than watching liberal Faux Reality programming. C-SPAN features secular humanists, ivory-tower East Coasters, freethinking progressive West Coasters, Europeans, poets who don't rhyme, and other pointy-headed, wine-swilling Homeland-haters who never have to make a payroll. Exposure to their ideas can make the entire pyramid, family, home, and Homeland collapse.

Certain substitutions are acceptable, however, on a temporary basis. In Figure F, the viewer is the Mommy. She has, because of hormones and domestic duties, replaced the Sports Group with the Home Shopping Channel. This change, while drastic, is acceptable because women are women and shopping supports the Homeland economy. This pyramid is acceptable only when the Mommy is alone. Once other members of the family are present and watching, viewing should revert to the ideal pyramid in Figure A.

FIGURE F

ARTICLE IV: THE TV VIEWING LOOKSEE

The UDA allows DOHD to view all cable and satellite TV company records to make certain that everyone's TV viewing is built solidly upon the Five Basic Building Blocks of Decent Viewing. Those records show who is watching what and whether it conforms to the Ideal Viewing Pyramid. Those whose TV-viewing pyramids are unhealthy and unbalanced will be contacted and told what programs will balance their viewing. Those who refuse to comply will have to report to DOHD regional centers to attend regular viewing sessions in which they will not have control of the TV remote.

ASK YOURSELF THIS!

Comedy is not one of the five basic DP TV viewing groups. That's because comedy usually does not support Homeland values. **Ask yourself this:** If you need humor in your life, what can you do to make sure there is wholesome, decent comedy during the Family Viewing Hour?

DOHD has the answer. Be part of the Family Programming Focus Panel. You could be one of the folks whose opinions are considered as we hone the Family Viewing Hour to include healthy, decency-affirming humor. Here are some of the programs we are working on. Perhaps you'll be one to give us the thumbs-up and a "Now, that's what I call funny!"

WE LOVE DADDY. A family show. Episode one has Mommy surprising Daddy with a pie on his birthday after Daddy bought her the new mixer she's been aching for. The hijinks surrounding the pie, the mixer, and Daddy's blond secretary are hilarious.

DATING THE DEVIL. A reality show. What do you think would happen if a woman got a job and ended up being the boss of fifteen men and dating all of them at the same time? Imagine the hilarity as she tries to keep all of their names and job responsibilities straight. The viewer gets to decide which ending is funnier: she's fired by the man above her; she gets pregnant and gets replaced; she gets a disease and gets replaced; or . . . you decide!

When Mommy doesn't submit to Daddy's benevolent authority, Intelligent Design becomes unbalanced. Children become confused: Sons grow up to be effeminate and daughters grow up to be feminist tomboys.

PRAYER, INTELLIGENT DESIGN, DECENCY, AND YOU

Our Intelligent Designer is smiling, because the forces of indecency are now on the defensive as the decent (those who are selected by the mysterious ways of Intelligent Design) move into positions of authority such as Congress, the Supreme Court, school boards, and, of course, DOHD, guaranteeing decent Homelanders the right to step into the light of day and shout, "Alleluia! We are right! Everyone else is wrong! Amen!"

ARTICLE I: ESTABLISHMENT OF PRAYER ZONES

DOHD has established a Floating Prayer Zone around everyone in which they can pray regardless of where they are. The Floating Prayer Zone is considered an extension of one's home and therefore can be used in public buildings, on public property, in schools, and at work. Anyone praying in a Floating Prayer Zone is protected because they are considered to be praying in their own home. No secular humanist, New Age musician, ACLU member, college professor, Clinton supporter, atheist, or the like may enter a Floating Prayer Zone unless asked in specifically for the purposes of repentance and conversion.

While in the Floating Prayer Zone, indecent words and ideas[31] are forbidden.

ARTICLE II: REQUIRED PRAYER AND RANDOM PRAYER

Prayer will be required in the Age of Decency. At first, prayers will be required only in the following situations: before and after meals; before doing "it" for divine help in obtaining successful impregnation; before government meetings, court sessions, big games, and job interviews; and in the classroom at the beginning and end of class. More will be added later as the level of decency in the Homeland warrants.

Random praying is not required and will not take the place of required prayers, but will be looked upon warmly by DOHD. Sudden bursts of prayer may occur anywhere at any time, whenever the mood strikes. Random praying may break out before filling out tax forms or after successful impregnation. Praising Intelligent Design for the pharmaceutical companies

---

[31]Examples of indecent words are: "Hillary Clinton," "endangered species list," "Koran," "tofu." Examples of indecent ideas are: evolution, Bill Moyers, President Hillary Clinton.

that make "it" possible for our seniors is an example of random praying. So is asking for divine help before merging onto a freeway so that if there is an accident, only indecent small hybrid foreign cars owned by liberals will be totaled.

ARTICLE III: THE GAG CLAUSE

DOHD, through the USA DECENCY ACT, has instituted the **God's Always Guaranteed to be there (GAG)** clause. Simply stated, GAG promotes the visibility of God in all areas of Homeland life: home, school, courthouses, police stations, firehouses, parks, sandboxes, dental offices, quarry pits, Senate chambers, governor's mansions, and so on. GAG legalizes the display of important religious documents inside and outside any public or private edifice. It also legalizes displays at or decoration of any public buildings to celebrate the Homeland's Christian traditions. This means "holiday" celebrations are banned but "Christmas" festivities are legal. Funding for such religious decoration and enforcement of pro-Christmas festivities may be financed by Decency Bake Sales, Decency 10Ks, and so on. (See Appendix C.)

GAG also establishes Permanent Prayer Zones[32] in all public buildings. Permanent Prayer Zones and established Prayer Times must be posted on all doors. GAG strongly encourages all companies, schools, hospitals, retail establishments, and so forth, to

[32]These are separate from Floating Prayer Zones and do not negate them. Everyone will continue to have Floating Prayer Zones, even in buildings with Permanent Prayer Zones, so everyone can pray wherever they wish.

pray before and after staff meetings and to base merit increases and raises on the fervency of each employee's praying style.

ARTICLE IV: EVERYTHING IS A CHURCH

The Church is wherever the decent gather and behave decently. This means the "Church" is sometimes the home, where the decent gather as a wholesome family to watch Fair and Balanced News shows or Pat Robertson, or where Mommy and Daddy retire after a hard day of work to express their love the Homeland Way: in the dark, silently, with the kids sound asleep so they don't know what is going on.

The following show how the Church is everywhere and thus must be allowed to be everywhere.

HOME. It is the Daddy's benevolent authority that makes his home a church. He is in charge and everyone must submit to his authority, because that is the plan of our Intelligent Designer (see Section I, Article I). The Daddy's benevolent authority is thus tested by the threat of eternal fire, and when Mommy doesn't submit to Daddy's benevolent authority, Intelligent Design becomes unbalanced. Children become confused: Sons grow up to be effeminate[33] and daughters may grow up to be feminist tomboys[34] who prefer baseball and lawyering to submitting to the benevolent authority of a man. Unsubmissive

[33]Or worse.
[34]Or worse.

Mommies also encourage Daddies to get in touch with their feminine side, which is expressly prohibited in many parts of the Bible and the Homeland.

SCHOOL. A school is decent, so a school is also a "church." That means teachers can say daily prayers before and after dealing with problem students, and students can say prayers before tests and lectures. Intelligent Design will eclipse evolution in schools/churches. (Those who continue to teach evolution will accompany those lessons with photos of monkeys and apes in unattractive poses in zoos, doing the things they usually do, like eating bananas and picking things off each other's heads.) The study of Intelligent Design will be accompanied by beautiful photos of God sitting on a cloud and pointing at the beautifulness of the Homeland.

BUSINESS. In the workplace, men and women are equals, but men are more so. As in the Bible, men were always the bosses, so the women went to the well to fill their buckets with water. Workplaces should reflect this to become "churches." This is also a good arena for teaching young single women about the benevolent authority of men. A middle-aged married man bossing around single female underlings by having them pick up his laundry or buying flowers for his spouse teaches young women what to look for in a husband and what to expect when they are married. In addition, incorporating prayer in daily business activities is especially important before closing big deals and before any Homeland audits.

GOVERNMENT. Political seats are like pews and should be treated with reverence, for politicians in the Homeland have a huge responsibility to the Homeland and its march backwards to the future (nowhere else is it so important to see prayer in action). God's point of view is enacted into law through government, so when politicians pray before debates or invoke God during Senate investigations or throughout presidential campaigns, Homelanders know they have nothing to fear from terrorists, abortion warehouses, stem-cell murderers, flag burners, and those who would soil the institution of marriage.

ARTICLE V: THE GOD LOOKSEE

The following is a list of DOHD's areas of concern. Further inquiries, fines, and punishments resulting from investigations of these concerns may be required and will be left to the discretion of each GAG agent who may conduct such inquiries and mete out such fines or punishments randomly, in secret, possibly in another country.

Prayer

GAG agents expect to see Homeland citizens praying before meals, and:

IN SCHOOLS. Before the Pledge of Allegiance, tests, big games, pep rallies, and during team huddles. Prayer in school is, at this time, vaguely illegal. Until prayer becomes compulsory, leeway will be given to those who pray silently, because they are not sure they should be praying at all.

IN THE WORKPLACE. Before meetings and conventions, during break-out groups, before and after slide presentations, in the washroom, by the watercooler, and before and after salary reviews. (DOHD rewards those businesses that find other excuses to make their employees pray during the workday.)

IN THE STADIUM OR THEATER. Before "The Star-Spangled Banner," before extra innings or sudden deaths, before the curtain goes up; after the applause, between acts, between commercials; for those in the penalty box or on the injured list; and when the fat lady sings.

IN GOVERNMENT OFFICES. Before convening or performing any governmental action. In addition, DOHD rewards lobbyists for especially fervent prayer before complex payoffs.

Prayers can be performed in a variety of ways, but GAG looks for the following:

Loud praying. Loud praying is proud praying.
Bent knee or prostrate praying. Uncomfortable praying is
    humble praying.

The composition of a prayer may be simple. Saying "Thank God" can be a sufficient prayer. (Not thanking God is rude and immoral. GAG agents take note of those who thank and give credit to God for winning games, raises, new jobs, Oscars, MTV awards, and doing "it" that results in successful conceptions.) Prayers may also be complex. Whatever is said is not as important as how loud and uncomfortable you are while you are saying it.

Religious Ornamentation

DOHD takes note of all homes and businesses that do not display Christmas decorations. Special allowances are made for Our Homeland Jews (**OHJs**) and others. What makes our Homeland special is that we recognize that OHJs and others should be able to live in our neighborhoods even if they do not believe in Jesus, Santa Claus, and the Easter Bunny. In the cases of OHJs and others, GAG places a special sticker on the front of said homes to let people know that there is a reason there is no Homeland Holiday ornamentation.

GAG also pays special attention to the kind of Homeland Holiday ornamentation displayed at each home. GAG likes to see (and sometimes requires) one or more of the following at each home or business:

MANGERS. Mangers must include the baby Jesus, Mary, Joseph, several barn animals, and hay. GAG will be lenient with mangers that make creative use of holiday symbols such as Santa Claus, gnomes, deer, sleighs, the seven dwarves, flamingos, and American flags. If Homeland homes lack some of the required manger features, they may use a suggested holiday symbol as a replacement. For instance, if there is no crib for the baby Jesus, it is acceptable for the baby Jesus to be held by a gnome or one of the seven dwarves, or placed on the back of a flamingo. If there are no typical manger animals, a herd of deer or a herd of flamingos is an acceptable substitute.[35]

LIGHTS. While lights are not strictly required, GAG approves of any lighting that makes it easier for it and DOHD to do their business. Lights also give the impression of pride and are a deterrent to terrorists who might consider breaking and entering during Homeland Holidays to steal our presents, our turkeys, our daughters, and our way of life. Lights may be strung on any part of the property of each home and business without regard to the number of lights or without regard to anyone else's feelings about the number of your lights or without regard to the fact that those bothered by said lights might be OHJs or others.

Religious Symbols and Paraphernalia

Until the Supreme Court finishes wrestling with separation of church and state, and until it finally becomes mandatory that GAG's provisions be applied in all areas of life, GAG agents will look for and quietly applaud God's symbols in all public spaces. The Ten Commandments should have places of honor in front of all courthouses, schools, government buildings, park entrances, Wal-Marts, orphanages, hospitals, sports arenas and airports,

---

[35]Special note on mangers: DOHD does not approve of and dislikes the use of the term "creche" when describing a manger. The word "creche" comes from France, where decency and God are still in hiding.

and any other public building according to the whim of GAG agents. Other religious symbols, overtly displayed, that meet with DOHD approval may include the following:

CRUCIFIXES. Especially when lit up or rigged with a motion sensor to play hymns when decent Homelanders walk by.

BIBLES. In hotels, hospitals, and government offices, and in creative spaces such as racetrack restrooms, grocery store magazine racks, abortion warehouses, and the like. Homeland homes should have at least one visible Bible (preferably situated so it can be seen through the front window by DOHD agents) and preferably one for each room in the house.

DOHD and GAG provisions, as well as common decency, require each Homeland citizen to seek approval of religious symbols that are not listed above before they are displayed in a public space.

HELPFUL TIPS

HOLIDAY EXPRESSIONS. DOHD disapproves of and will eventually be able to fine and or punish those who water down holiday expressions. Substituting any of the following for "Merry Christmas" is considered suspect: "Happy Holidays," "Peace," "Season's Greetings," "Happy Tree Day," "Here's to Your Elves," "No Nukes," and so on. Remember to write "Merry Christmas" on all your holiday correspondence and say it when greeting people during the Christmas season.

SPREADING GOD AND DECENCY. It behooves all Homeland citizens to mention God whenever and wherever they can. DOHD suggests that each citizen use every opportunity to express their faith by creatively exploiting openings in conversations at cocktail parties, baby showers, business meetings, and the like.

The following is an example that may help you in these situations:

"Hey, Sarah, could you hand me some of that clam dip?"

"Sure thing, Ted. Say, aren't clams one of God's cutest creations?"

"Boy, Sarah, I never thought about it before. How about that herring? Is that one of God's jokes?"

"Oh, Ted, I never thought about it like that. Ha! Ha! Let's take our dip and herring over to the couch and talk some more!"

The Homeland came to
an important decision:

Breasts in general
should never be seen
or talked about.

THE HOMELAND CONVERSATION

HOMELANDERS LOVE HOMELAND CONVERSATIONS

After sitting around watching a Fair and Balanced News show on hot topics of the day, Homelanders love to discuss what they have just been told is true with their family and friends.

This is how we grow decency—through Homeland Conversations. In the early days of the Homeland, these discussions used to be held around a hearty dinner table groaning with big pieces of meat. But, unlike today's conversations, those conversations tended to be unfocused and often touched on difficult subjects, like why their teenaged babysitter had to go visit her aunt for nine months. The mother and father did not have the advantage of expert pundits to help them answer those questions in a way that did not tell their children more than they should know, which is nothing.

ARTICLE 1: FAIR AND BALANCED NEWS SHOWS WILL SET CONVERSATION AGENDAS

National conversations will take place whenever an important issue arises and is discussed nonstop on our many Fair and Balanced News shows. The Homeland is fortunate to have so many twenty-four-hour news channels and outlets like YouTube that are so eager to lead us in these conversations.

We've had many of these opportunities in recent years, touching on subjects such as whether a Muslim elected to Congress is necessarily a traitor, why universal health care is a godless communist activist idea that won't work, and whether people take charity because they have weak characters or because they are all just lazy bums.[36]

These can serve as examples of the kind we will have in the future, although all future conversations will be mandatory. One such conversation reached a national consensus that even though Homelanders might be racist and sexist, decent Homelanders were not as racist and sexist as hip-hop artists. This was a breakthrough, for now Homelanders feel better about themselves knowing that they are not the only racists and sexists and, if they are, they probably learned it from somebody else, such as those youth who play music loudly on their car radios.

---

[36]National consensus: yes.

Decent neighborhoods and decent drivers exposed to loud rap and hip-hop on car radios become confused by the indecent lyrics and the loud bass, and this might be where some Homelanders learn some of these racist and sexist ideas and then assume they are acceptable.[37]

Another useful example of a Homeland Conversation is the horrific period in Homeland History known as the Janet Jackson Super Bowl Halftime Wardrobe Malfunction. Because of that totally planned indecency, innocent children all across the Homeland believed the lie that your clothes can fall off if they feel like it.

A national consensus had to be reached quickly. Sound television pundits worked overtime to figure out what facts the Homeland needed to make a wise decision: Covered breasts are OK; uncovered breasts are disgusting; jewelry on breasts is so indecent, it shouldn't be talked about. And Super Bowl halftime entertainment should be monitored closely if anyone other than Andy Williams performs.

ARTICLE II: EVERYONE WILL PARTICIPATE IN ALL HOMELAND CONVERSATIONS

In order for Homeland Conversations to be powerful and reach decent consensus, everyone will be involved. Conversations may take place at the dinner table (preferably with hearty meaty

---

[37]As we march proudly backwards to the future, we will not have that problem, because all music that can't be played in elevators and shopping malls will be strongly discouraged with fines.

entrées), in town halls, around the water cool, in locker rooms—wherever Homelanders can gather, with the obvious exception of restrooms, both public and private, where it is in the Homeland's best interest that the Homeland's "business" be completed as quickly and quietly as possible.

Neighborhood Decency Posses (NDP) will facilitate all conversations to make sure no one goes off topic or criticizes the President and that the correct consensus is reached. Attendance during public conversations is mandatory and will be taken.[38] Attendance at conversations around the dinner table is on the honor system. It is expected that the Homeland husband will mete out discipline for missed conversations. A surprise national conversation LookSee should be expected at homes.

ARTICLE III: ALL CONVERSATIONS
WILL BE RECORDED

NDP facilitators will write down or tape-record everything that is said during national conversations.[39] These notes and tapes will be forwarded to DOHD headquarters, where the responses will be analyzed so that a national consensus can be reached. During these analyses, any comments deemed indecent or unenthusiastic will be brought to the attention of the local NDP,

---

[38]Those absent from a public Homeland conversation will need a doctor's note explaining the medical necessity for that absence and will also submit a complete copy of their medical records going back ten years.

[39]In cases where NDP facilitators are called away to handle Homeland emergencies, the conversation in that location must stop immediately. Participants may discuss the weather—but not global warming—until the facilitator returns.

which will take action as necessary. Please refer to Appendix A: Proscribed Punishments for what can happen to you if you cause our Homeland Conversation to falter or reach a consensus that is obscene, unsound, anti-God, or remotely activist.

ARTICLE IV: CONVERSATIONS WILL HAVE SYMBOLIC PROPS AND GUIDELINES

SYMBOLIC PROPS. Flags must be waved freely and often during Homeland Conversations. A flag is just another way of saying "Amen!" DOHD prefers that all flags be made in the Homeland, unless a Homeland corporation finds it more advantageous to have those flags manufactured cheaply in sweatshops in foreign countries or by elderly shut-ins (who need to earn some pocket change to pay for their prescription medications). Plastic lapel pins may also be worn, although these should not be waved for fear of exposing an indecent body part and tainting the minds of young Homelanders.

GUIDELINES. Homeland Conversations will begin and end with prayer. Prayers will ask for sound wisdom and understanding as well as for the ability to look into the hearts of those who seem uncooperative or indecent while conversing. Conversations will be positive and uplifting. Since these conversations are often about horrific indecencies too indecent to describe, no one should describe them.

The following examples should help to keep conversations short in order to minimize embarrassment and discomfort.

Homosexual Homeland Conversation

NDP Facilitator: Do you think homosexual people can be turned into nonhomosexual people?

Homelander: Yes.

Islamism Homeland Conversation

NDP Facilitator: What are benefits for women who wear burkas, and should Homeland women think about wearing them, too?

Homelander: What's a burka? Is that the Muslim word for parka? Isn't it too hot in those countries with deserts to wear parkas? Can burkas fall off like Janet Jackson's shirt? If not, maybe all women should wear them.

In cases where a Homelander misses a Homeland Conversation or has no family or friends or neighbors or coworkers to have a conversation with AND an NDP facilitator cannot be present, the Homelander will be required to hold a personal Homeland Conversation with themselves.

For example:

Equal Pay for Equal Work Conversation

Homelander, to himself: Why don't women earn as much as men?

Homelander, answering himself: Because women's hormones make them less employable and not as good at their jobs.

Homelander, replying to his own answer: That's right.

Age of the Earth Conversation

Homelander, to himself: How old is the earth?

Homelander, answering himself: Millions of years?

Homelander, chastising himself: No, stupid. Six thousand years old.

Solo Homeland Conversations must be recorded and sent to DOHD headquarters, where they will be analyzed and added to the national consensus on a per-month basis. Solo conversations that do not agree with the national consensus will be submitted to the proper DOHD authorities and investigated.

HOMELAND CONVERSATION LOOKSEE

DOHD agents will make surprise checks on all Homeland Conversations, including Solo Homeland Conversations. They will take special notice of those who:

ARE NOT ENJOYING THE CONVERSATION. Does the participant eagerly wave his arm AND his flag, or does he slump in his chair and gripe about the lack of granola on the Homeland Conversation breakfast menu?

ARRIVE LATE WITH AN INDECENT EXCUSE. When a citizen arrives late to a Homeland Conversation, a DOHD official should determine the cause. Was said resident late because he was busy picketing an abortion factory? Does he ask if he missed the prayer and, if so, could they repeat the prayer for his sake? Does the citizen ride his bicycle to the meeting hall without considering the lack of bike racks, as befits a just and trustworthy four-wheel-drive society?

STRIKE CONTROVERSY AND THEREFORE INTERFERE WITH PEACEFUL HOMELAND DIALOGUE. While all citizens—including the Homeland's worst—are required to attend Homeland Conversations, occasionally rebels will try to disrupt the dialog with foreign ideas or yell liberal slogans solely to disrupt and disturb the peaceful crowd. Unacceptable epithets include:

- Do "it," not war!
- Give (Organic) Peas a Chance
- 6 Billion Miracles Is Enough
- Soy Bomb

Until complete Homeland consensus is reached on all subjects, there will always be rebels and the need for DOHD vigilance. Those who refuse to comply with Homeland Conversation guidelines will be required to have multiple One-on-One Homeland Conversations with a DOHD agent at a location that DOHD does not have to tell you about. Such conversations will continue until they sound like this:

DOHD Agent: Are you going to ride your bicycle to a Homeland
   Conversation ever again?
Homelander: No.

For conversations that do not follow and conclude as the previous example, please refer to Appendix A: Proscribed Punishments.

ASK YOURSELF THIS!

Are you decent but shy? Are you excited about the idea of Homeland Conversations but are afraid to speak up? DOHD, in partnership with Homeland pharmaceutical giants who sponsor many of our Fair and Balanced News programs, want to take part in forming the Homeland consensus. There are medications, tested at least once before FDA approval, that may help you overcome your shyness. These medications have some side effects (including dry mouth, fatigue, and death), but nothing can outweigh the feeling of having helped decide that, say, walls do make good neighbors and that, if building one on our Mexican border is a good idea, so is building one on our Canadian border. As long as you (and your family and their heirs and their heirs) agree in writing never to file a frivolous lawsuit against the Homeland drug company who manufactures your medication, you could be just a pill away from full participation in a Homeland Conversation.

Naps are never a good leisure idea, because they are often done lying down, which leads to any number of indecent isms.

HOMELAND FUN AND LEISURE

The Homeland never takes a decency break, but Homelanders sometimes need to rest and reboot their strength and conviction. Vigilance can take a toll on even the most robust among us: How can we wind down, but not completely unwind in our windup to defeating the terrorists at our back door?

One way to keep decency robust is to relax and have fun.

Can decent people have fun? Yes, but be very careful. There is fun and there is "fun."[40] Homelanders need to be wary of the difference between the two. Taking your children to a movie about animals can be fun or it can be "fun."[41] A family vacation to a

---

[40] "Fun" can be just as bad a word as that which "it" describes. In fact, sometimes "fun" is "it." It is crucial that if you are going to have fun, make sure it is fun and not "fun."

[41] Animal movies or cartoons often use a secret code where the characters, like penguins or crabs, raise their children in unnatural settings without both a Mommy and Daddy and promote unsound science, earth-warming messages, or dancing as a way of life for men.

theme park can be fun or it can be "fun."[42] Having the wrong kind of fun can put your family on the dangerous and slippery slope to hedonism, liberalism, environmentalism, anti-consumerism, anti-meatism, and all the rest of the isms that there are more of every day. No wonder we need some relaxation! Decency—fighting off the onslaught of isms—takes work!

DOHD believes that fun and decency can coexist in the household. Using a panel of experts (theme park managers, gym teachers, faith-based leisure experts, snowmobile enthusiasts, and the like), DOHD has set guidelines for low-risk leisure activities that can provide the correct amount of rest and relaxation and the right kind of fun. Please pay close attention so as not to jeopardize future leisure opportunities.

ARTICLE I: LEISURE ACTIVITIES
ARE QUICK ACTIVITIES

No matter what type of leisure a Homelander chooses, it should be over quickly. DOHD recommends no more than two hours per weekend for Sedentary Leisure (e.g., hobbies and crafts), and a maximum of one week (Monday to Sunday) for Mobile Leisure (e.g., family vacations, hunting).

DOHD has determined that any further time spent engaging in either of the two acceptable types of leisure leads to sloth and a reduction in our firmness and potency as a productive nation.

---

[42]For example, there is a major theme park associated with a big-eared mouse that has a special day for OHFs. That day will be avoided by all decent Homelanders.

The only exception to this rule is for CEOs and corporate offi-cers, as their professional lives are more important and there-fore more exhausting than the rest of ours.

ARTICLE II: LEISURE IS NOT AN ENTITLEMENT

Leisure should not be subsidized by others. It must be earned, which means paid for by the Homelander out of the Home-lander's own leisure nest egg. Leisure without personal respon-sibility (i.e., paid for by someone else like your boss) is hazardous to the Homeland economy. Leisure paid for out of your own pocket also ensures adherence to Article I.

Again, the only acceptable subsidized leisure is for CEOs and other officers of large corporations. Because they work so hard to provide meaningful and lasting employment for Home-landers and support DOHD in its work to keep the workplace decent, their boards of directors shall pay for their leisure.

ARTICLE III: WHAT HOMELAND LEISURE IS

Homeland Leisure, first and foremost, takes place in the Home-land.

Children are included in all family leisure activities.[43] Because the majority of Homeland Leisure opportunities are also learning

---

[43]Having fun without their children may remind a Homeland couple of how much fun their lives were before having children. This is counterproductive to the Homeland Way, which is having more children, not less.

moments, you may think of the family vacation or the family sitting around the television as another way of homeschooling. Additionally, hiring a babysitter to watch your children is risky, because most babysitters are teenagers and most teenagers are steaming cauldrons of hormones that can spill out and infect your children.

Homeland leisure should be something you are not embarrassed to have your neighbors see through your front window. Nor should your neighbors hear anything associated with indecent language or loud discussions over Homeland policy. Such time-wasters are best left to policy makers and deciders who know better than you do.

ARTICLE IV: WHAT HOMELAND LEISURE IS NOT

Homeland Leisure does not take place in places like France or Mexico or other countries crippled by vacation policies that allow employees to take a month or more off every year. Business and industry in places that shut down in the middle of the day for several hours so workers can have long lunches and naps and indecent "fun"are also strictly forbidden. DOHD does not believe in long lunches or naps. Fast food was invented for a good reason: to keep lunches focused and short, workers productive, and temptations at bay. Naps are never a good idea, because they are often done lying down, which leads to any number of indecent isms.

ARTICLE V: THE TWO TYPES OF
HOMELAND LEISURE

Sedentary Leisure

Sedentary Leisure is any type of leisure activity than can be done sitting in a chair, or can be managed without taking more than a few steps in order to fully enjoy the relaxation needed from that activity.[44]

Sedentary Leisure is permitted during the weekday, as long as it is at night, does not conflict with work or child rearing, and takes place in front of the television (men and women) or in the garage (men only). Sedentary Leisure is permitted during the weekend, provided there are no conflicts with faith-based activities.

APPROVED TYPES OF SEDENTARY LEISURE: CRAFTS AND HOBBIES

Crafts are commonly the domain of women, because they involve delicate work that a man's large manly hands cannot do. These include activities like scrapbooking, knitting, and recipe clipping.

Although not required, it is a good idea if all craft projects have a purpose other than just fun. Knitting can be relaxing, but

---

[44]Spending more than two hours in a chair has been found to induce useless daydreaming, uncontrolled fantasies, and inclinations to engage in unapproved forms of "it." Doing "it" is not considered decent if it involves sitting in a chair. Doing "it" in a chair is the kind of "fun" that also can lead to accidents and the possibility of your neighbors seeing you, which would be the case since your living room windows should always have shades and curtains wide open to facilitate LookSees and Decency Posse Patrols.

it can also be the difference between a husband who is chilly and ineffectual or warm and ruthlessly efficient. Dual-purpose crafts include coupon sorting, towel monogramming, lampshade decoupage, Christmas centerpiece–making, and anything that prepares the family for Homeland holidays. DOHD encourages women to come up with appropriate leisure crafts that can be done with attention to family, to the television program her family is watching while she is doing her craft, and to the craft itself.

Hobbies can be enjoyed by both men and women and should have a similar dual purpose. If you are a man and you have a gun collection, clean and polish it while sitting in the living room with the rest of the family during Family Viewing Hour on television. If your hobby is something that can be done only in the garage, it is acceptable to excuse yourself from the family and go tinker. Tinkering is a male activity—it is a good way for strong men to bond, as it involves tools that are too large for women's delicate hands. Decent men enjoy watching and advising other men as they tinker, or just staring vacantly at tools and mechanical objects.

Other enjoyable male hobbies include trimming his Homeland shrubbery and spraying the yard for weeds. Remember, the man who says "My yard is my hobby!" is the man who has used his leisure to beautify and purge his neighborhood. DOHD rewards those Homelanders who are unselfish with their fun.

Be wary of using your Sedentary Leisure when enjoying the arts (e.g., listening to music, reading books, watching movies). Elsewhere in this manual, DOHD is very specific about what does and does not constitute decent arts and literature.

Mobile Leisure

Mobile Leisure involves activities outside the home that require movement or a recreational vehicle. Whether it is hunting or fishing, paintball or war reenactments, KOA camping or a week spent exploring Precious Moments sites and county fairs, Mobile Leisure activities will energize your family and the Homeland as well.

Sports make excellent Mobile Leisure activities. Sports prepare the Homeland male by teaching him that winning is everything and that the team is merely an extension of the Army of Decency that is marching us proudly backwards to the future with the ball.

Women may participate in sports like softball, where the ball is big and unlikely to hurt or disfigure them, but not in sports like volleyball, where participants may be required to wear indecent clothing like bikinis.

Contrary to what other countries may have you believe, certain sports are not really sports and should not be discussed or indulged in at the risk of confusing American youth. These nonsports include polo, croquet, and any other physical activity where the clothing is feminine or tea is drunk afterward. Real sports require sweating, scoring that makes sense, and domestic beer or Gatorade, not tea.

Vacations are also ideal Mobile Leisure outlets, and there are numerous opportunities for a vacation to be both relaxing and educational. Whatever vacation you decide to take with your family, do your Homeland automobile and petroleum industries a favor: Buy or rent a large recreational vehicle, possibly one large enough to tow an SUV for family side trips. Doing so allows your family members to travel in utmost comfort and style, and lets you bring your television with you so the kids don't miss Family Viewing Hour on TV.

One of DOHD's favorite vacation ideas is the family camping trip. What better way to remind you of the beauty of our own Homeland? It's a healthy reminder that our Intelligent Designer favored us above all other nations, and that we should show our thanks by continuing to contribute to Homeland economy and industry. And what better way than camping is there to provide memorable teaching moments for Homeland children? Camping can be a son's introduction to shooting small game like chipmunks and sparrows, and a daughter's introduction to cooking food a man has provided.[45] Sitting around the campfire is also a fun way to teach your children decent songs that make sense and are not about "it." The campfire is a place to learn "Kumbaya," not "Lay, Lady, Lay."

In addition, the campfire can teach valuable lessons about the real facts of forestry: Contrary to what activist tree-huggers say, trees grow back right away,[46] and if it is OK to use them in a Leisure Activity, it is certainly OK to use them in industry as well.

Not all camping is decent. Wilderness camping is for loners who are selfish about their leisure. While it is important to see nature to understand why man is in charge of it, too much

---

[45]Guns can be brought on all family vacations and gun racks can be adapted to all sorts of vehicles, not just RVs and pickups. The clever gun-owner can attach a gun rack to a bicycle, a canoe, Jet Skis, and so on. A gun rack can be attached to the family dog, regardless of its size. For additional ideas, DOHD can send you a copy of "How to Mount a Gun Rack Anywhere at All."

[46]Or whenever the Intelligent Designer wants them to.

nature leads to communing with nature, and communing[47] with nature can lead to prurient activities like skinny-dipping and doing "it" in dirt. Wilderness camping also requires traveling light, negating the use of giant coolers filled with enormous amounts of meat and beer that support the Homeland's food industry. If you are in doubt about the kind of camping you are doing, look around: If you see lots of plug-ins for campers and lots of pavement and gravel rock, you're in a safe place that clearly looks out for the comfort of visiting Homelanders. If you see thick brush, random dirt and rock, and bearded solo campers, your family is at risk of catching an STD.[48] Immediately relocate your family somewhere safe (such as a McDonald's, which are conveniently located near all decent campgrounds) and contact DOHD authorities, who will send agents to clear the area and mark it as a site for future paved development.

THE LEISURE LOOKSEE

Besides monitoring Homelanders to see whether they are having fun or "fun," DOHD is especially interested in leisure that benefits the community at large. DOHD agents will consider participation in the following leisure activities as a sign of allegiance to both the health of the Homelander and the Homeland:

ARCHAEOLOGICAL DIGS. Did you know you can now go to an excavation site and learn what sound science has always told us

[47]Derived from the word "Communist," a way of life that we destroyed and a word that will eventually be struck from all dictionaries.
[48]Socially Transmitted Derangement.

was true: that dinosaurs and men are all the same age—about six thousand years old—and that man invented fire so their wives could cook dinosaur steaks? If your family cannot afford a pilgrimage to one of these historical sites, the Internet is a fine place to explore Creationist Digs for the whole family.

SHOOTING RANGES. Because the indecent have always had guns, and because all decent fathers and sons will be required to carry them, too, a vacation that incorporates a shooting range can be more than just fun: It is a place where sharpshooting techniques and assault-weapon skills necessary for Homeland survival can be honed. Women and daughters are welcome, as long as they bring sandwiches, sit on chairs at a distance, and offer praise.

BRANSON AND PLACES LIKE IT. Branson hearkens to a time when the Homeland was pure. Many great, decent entertainers from the past live on and perform there, some dead (and played by impersonators) and some not as dead (with impersonators ready to take over when they are). DOHD loves when families go to places like Branson, because DOHD agents on LookSee duty then have an excuse to hear Andy Williams, a decent performer who can really rev up anyone's decency motor!

FAMILY BIBLE CAMP. Without exception, DOHD agents will approve of any Homelander who chooses Bible camp as their yearly vacation destination.

During the Leisure LookSee, agents will pay particular attention to those Homelanders who look like they are having too much fun and immediately approach the individual Homelander or the family and say one of the following: "OK, the fun's over!" or "OK, you've had your fun!" Under no circumstances will an agent tolerate the following responses: "Hey, the fun's just starting!" or "Are we having fun yet?" Such rejoinders do not convey the respect for hardworking DOHD officers or the decent heritage of our ancestors.

ASK YOURSELF THIS!

Grand Canyon National Park is now required to have literature explaining how the Grand Canyon was formed—either by an Intelligent Designer who was smart and did things fast, or by evolution, which is not smart and goes really slow. **Ask yourself this:** In what other leisure destinations would you like to see facts corrected, or at least have both sides of the story presented (even though one side is obviously wrong and godless)? Do you believe, as most decent Homelanders do, that Noah's flood created all the national parks? And what about museums? Would you like to see legends next to bones and tools and pottery changed to their real age, or allow indecent scientists to concoct pseudoscientific theories in order to advance their secular humanist agendas? You can help DOHD by sending us the names of those places where you believe an artifact's age has been misinterpreted. But until we can correct the situation, visit these places at your own risk.

Words lead to ideas,
which are the saplings of indecency.

Pretty soon you have a forest that
needs to be burned to the ground.

THE GLOSSARY OF INDECENCY

WARNING!

CHILDREN AND SENSITIVE ADULTS SHOULD AVOID THIS GLOSSARY. ALTHOUGH THEY NEED ACCESS TO THE INFORMATION CONTAINED HEREIN, IT IS BETTER THAT IT IS DISSEMINATED TO THEM BY A MEMBER OF THEIR NEIGHBORHOOD DECENCY POSSE WITH SOUND EXPERIENCE IN ICKY SUBJECTS. THOSE WHO IGNORE THIS WARNING SHOULD NOT EXPECT THEIR INSURANCE TO COVER RESULTING PSYCHOLOGICAL PROBLEMS.

Life was originally meant to be lived without ever coming into contact with words like "bootylicious," "evolution," or even "it." And that is how life will be lived in the future as we complete our proud march backwards to that time.

But until the glorious day of complete decency dawns, Homelanders must vigilantly protect themselves against disgustingly wayward words and thoughts. Just as a decent Homelander might not want to try hummus offered by an immigrant coworker in the employee lunchroom, a decent Homelander does not want to use words such as "hummus" when there are better and more decent words like "dip." Words lead to ideas, which are the saplings of indecency. Pretty soon you have a forest that needs to be burned to the ground. Remember, throughout history, decent people were always people of few and decent words, just as Gary Cooper and John Wayne portrayed them before liberals took over and ruined Hollywood.

The following is a list of words that will no longer be used in the Homeland. Homelanders will be required to use their synonyms, which follow each definition. The list is relatively short now, but will expand as DOHD language experts have the stomach to work on it. Homelanders will be expected to update themselves yearly.

ALTERNATIVE FORMS OF ENERGY The form of energy preferred by Satanists; also, a direct assault on the profit structure of decent Homeland businesses like British Petroleum, which could lead to many people freezing to death in winter or being unable to get to their vacation spots in summer because of high gasoline prices. Acceptable synonyms: pie in the sky, genocide, treasonous, special interests.

ARTIST One who contributes nothing wholesome to society; a degenerate who sleeps late, lives in subsidized lofts, and wants the state to pay lots for his product. Acceptable synonyms: drunkard, drug addict, leech, homosexual.

ATHEIST Literally without God, morals, or friends. Hated by most Homelanders. Seeks to take over the public square for the purposes of promoting atheism. Wants to romp in the forests with the children of decent Homelanders in order to recruit them to their godless cult. Acceptable synonyms: terrorist, enemy of the state, homosexual.

BITCH A woman who effortlessly makes life miserable for men. A woman who argues, doesn't cook, and would rather work than stay at home. Acceptable synonyms: God's test, God's joke, God's mistake.

BOOTYLICIOUS Having the quality of shapeliness in a bodily area that inspires indecency in good men everywhere. Soft and desirable, but slightly slutty curvaceousness in a woman that is best concealed with loose clothing. A tender feminine area that makes strong men think twice about settling down and keeping the Homeland safe from indecencies. Acceptable synonyms: bad thought, home-wrecking slut feature.

BRA BURNING A hippie act of rebellion against all that was decent and good in the Homeland. The act of loosing upon the world vulgar forces that should remain tied down. The first step down the slippery slope to breast-feeding in public areas. Acceptable synonyms: feminism, lesbianism, atheism, witchery.

CANADA A country that is too much like France and too close for the Homeland's comfort. May have invented hockey and produced Loren Greene and Celine Dion, but also contains Quebec and is a vacation destination for indecent Vermonters. Acceptable synonym: pacifist Frenchie wannabes.

DERRIERE A French word no one needs to know. Acceptable synonyms: caboose, bottom, rear end.

ENVIRONMENTALIST A mental case, possibly the anti-Christ. One who places trees and frogs above the welfare of Homeland jobs and children. As useful as a tick. Would kill you and your family to save a tick. Acceptable synonym: elitist, blood-engorged, disease-carrying tick.

EVOLUTION The denial of all things good and decent. A theory that says your mother is a monkey, your children are monkeys, you are a monkey, the President is a monkey, and morals are just so much monkey business. Acceptable synonyms: monkey business, unsound science, sacrilege.

FEMINISM A dangerous movement that wants all men killed. Members must never shave, kill their husbands, wear underwear only if they feel like it, kill their boyfriends, have full control over their bodies, kill men randomly, take all the jobs that were meant for men, and kill all the men left. Acceptable synonym: loud hairy slut-ism.

GLBT (pronounced: guh-luh-buh-tuh) A dirty word that fortunately no one knows how to pronounce. An unnatural movement about unnatural "it," unnatural surgery, unnatural wardrobes, and unnatural dancing (because no one knows who is supposed to lead). Acceptable synonyms: icky (ik-ee), hell-bound (hel-bownd).

GLOBAL WARMING A scare tactic created by activist weather-men. An impotent swearword that elitist, blood-engorged, disease-carrying ticks use to turn the natural phenomena that the Intelligent Designer clearly intended (the normal melting of the ice caps, the warming of the earth so we can grow more genetically engineered crops all year-round, anywhere at all, even the North Pole) into an immature, reactionist children's bedtime story. Acceptable synonyms: a blessing, progress.

GREENHOUSE GAS The noxious stuff that comes out of environmentalists and vegans. Acceptable synonym: the fart of terrorists.

HILLARY The most dangerous person in America. Do not use this word. If this word comes up in a conversation and you can't leave, cover your ears and make shrill sounds until the danger passes. Acceptable synonyms: none.

HIP-HOP A term co-opted from the sacred Homeland Easter Bunny tradition that now refers to music from drug gangs, prison gangs, college student gangs, and godless slackers who illegally download music on the interweb for free. Acceptable synonym: loud music that no one understands except gang members.

HO   Another co-opted term from a sacred Homeland Holiday. Once part of Santa's greeting, it now means a woman of easy virtue who does "it" all the time. Acceptable synonym: Ho! Ho! Ho! (three times), as long as you are chubby and dressed in a red suit. All other synonyms: nonmarriage material.

INTELLECTUAL Hater of common sense, sound science, and the Intelligent Designer. Acceptable synonyms: traitor, deviant, godless liberal, East Coast pervert.

MULTICULTURALISM Disgusting philosophy that four cultures are better than three cultures, which are better than two cultures, all of which are better than the one decent culture. Supported by haters, traitors, intellectuals, liberals, and people who learn more than the one officially decent language. Sometimes known as Diversity. Acceptable synonyms: melting cesspool, the destruction of decency, hummus activism.

NATALIE MAINES The second-most-dangerous person in America; traitor; atheist; liberal. Any Homelander who has any Dixie Chicks CDs should either drive over them with a Hummer (DOHD scientists have determined that the weight and power of only a Hummer will completely destroy a Dixie Chicks CD) or send them to DOHD, where we will replace them with a free Celine Dion poster. Acceptable synonyms: vulgar excuse for a woman, rendition candidate.

ORGANIC Any food that is disease ridden, moldy, and full of dirt. Grown, sold, and eaten by liberal elitist activists. Acceptable synonym: laxative.

PILL A product of unsound science and an excuse to do "it" willy-nilly. Caused extreme confusion and bitterness for men because of the expression "on the Pill," which loose feminist women determined to mean that women now had the freedom to be "on top." Acceptable synonym: evil loud hairy slut candy.

PLANNED PARENTHOOD A house of ill repute, where baby haters dole out contraceptives like candy on Halloween. Run by feminist, bra-burning sluts. Acceptable synonym: Loud Hairy Slut, Inc.

PROFESSOR One who professes false beliefs and never had to meet a payroll. One who knows much useless information. Anyone who reads too much, listens to NPR, watches public TV, or hates *American Idol*. Acceptable synonym: tedious bore.

SIXTIES Decade when the Homeland was overrun with hippies, hedonists, malcontents, protesters, liberals, Communists, antiwar activists, sit-ins, teach-ins, and homosexual recruiting. The free-speech movement got its start, war became unpopular, and foreign cars grew popular among certain groups of Homeland haters, like college students. Acceptable synonyms: none. Because it was such a blotch on the Homeland History, this decade has been expunged. The Fifties now go to 1965, after which the Seventies begin immediately.

STREISAND, BARBRA The third-most-dangerous person in America. A Hollywood liberal whose records or CDs should all be destroyed. Send them to DOHD and we will send you a free autographed poster of Ted Nugent field-dressing a deer he just shot (and be sure to catch his brand-new, action-packed music video of this very hunt, available at better gun shows everywhere). Acceptable synonym: funny girl slut.

VEGANS Holier-than-thou PETA types who always get sick and die in their early fifties. Self-hating, indecent hippies who shun eggs and milk so that they can catch painful diseases that could have been cured by a good meat-and-potatoes diet. Acceptable synonyms: nuts, fools, malnourished morons, homosexuals.

If you are indecent, it will hurt.

The more indecent you are,
the more it will hurt.

The most indecent are punished in
another country
(e.g., Egypt, Turkey, the Vatican)
at Homeland taxpayers' expense.

It will hurt the most.

PROSCRIBED PUNISHMENTS

DOHD believes that punishment is the best way to knock decency into the indecent, especially the most stubbornly indecent. Like a child who misbehaves, the indecent man (or woman) will continue his bad behavior until someone slaps him across the room or into the next county. And, as with children, DOHD believes that corporal punishment fits the crime in all cases. However, there are levels of severity in corporal punishment, so in all cases, no matter the severity, remember DOHD's motto on the subject: "It's not how much it hurts, but for how long afterward."[49]

While it would seem helpful to know what the punishments

---

[49]DOHD is devising more mottoes all the time, for all occasions. Mottoes help decent Homelanders remember the rules of decency.

are, and the severity of punishment for each level of crime, DOHD likes to keep this kind of thing secret, just because it can.

You need to know only the following:

> If you are indecent, it will hurt.
> The more indecent you are, the more it will hurt.
> The most indecent are punished in another country
> (e.g., Egypt, Turkey, the Vatican)
> at Homeland taxpayers' expense.
> It will hurt the most.

"IF YOU HAVE NOTHING TO FEAR . . ."

Corporal punishment may be accompanied—according to the whim and the mood of the punisher—by humiliation, which is defined as: asking really personal questions, counseling, intervention, exorcism, ridicule, bribery, payoffs, showing pictures of "it," confiscation of personal property (such as television remotes, wives, daughters, lawn mowers, and any other precious Homeland items DOHD deems fit).

While DOHD punishment can change the indecent back to the decent, it can be frightening. The best and only way to avoid severe DOHD punishment is to strive for decency and remain decent and to remember this DOHD motto:

> You have nothing to fear
> if you have nothing to hide.

You have nothing to hide
if you have nothing to fear.

So fear nothing
and you need not hide.

Hide nothing
and you need not fear.

If it looks like a duck,
talks like a duck,
walks like a duck,
does "it" like a duck,
votes Green Party,
likes Jon Stewart,
buys free-range eggs,
is childless by choice,
and uses a push mower,
it's a duck
and it must be reported.

STARTING YOUR OWN
NEIGHBORHOOD DECENCY POSSE

A neighborhood is only as decent as the least decent person living in it. You may not drink French wines, watch PBS, or read the *Village Voice,* but if your neighbor does you are tainted by mere proximity. Proximity to indecency is only a tweak away from your family doing "it" with animals, having abortions willy-nilly, and inviting terrorists over for a barbecue. Chaos and indecency will reign.

DOHD, while always vigilant and always concerned, cannot be in all places at all times. The establishment of Neighborhood Decency Posses fills this void and can be of great service when an official DOHD LookSee cannot be performed. You can be the ears and eyes of DOHD. In the unending war against indecency, you can be the tape recorder, the microphone, the binoculars, and, yes, in the event of extreme indecency, the gun.

In addition to general neighborhood spying for the Homeland, a Posse Member can be posted to the following areas:

- Day care centers
- School libraries
- Public libraries
- Locker rooms
- Poetry readings
- Abortion warehouses
- Vermont

HOW TO START YOUR OWN
NEIGHBORHOOD DECENCY POSSE

1. Before you can start your own Neighborhood Decency Posse, you must complete the Neighborhood Decency Posse Quiz (at the end of this appendix). Once you have passed this quiz, proceed to step 2 below.

2. Identify those in your neighborhood who are decent, courageous men. You can use this manual to determine the decency of all men who live or work near you.[50] Those men you find to form a Posse must, like you, have passed the NDP Quiz.

3. Set up your first NDP meeting. A Posse meeting includes these DOHD-approved elements: recitation of the new Pledge

---

[50]Women cannot be part of Neighborhood Decency Posses. While they can be decent, they lack the strength and courage to take part in activities that could be dangerous. And because of their rampant hormones, they are easy prey for the indecent and other terrorists. Their place should be at home, protecting the children, power tools, television remotes, and other precious Homeland property.

of Allegiance, where "under God" will be mentioned five times; a Secret Posse Handshake or other unity-building Posse tool; distribution of Posse equipment, including walkie-talkies, flashlights, sunglasses, binoculars, clipboards, fake noses, and official DOHD hats, windbreakers, and stain-resistant Dockers made especially for DOHD.[51]

4. At the initial Posse meeting, "Posse Buddies" are established. The Buddy System is used to prevent indecent people from getting the advantage over a sole Posse Member. An Al Franken joke or a bawdy Britney Spears comment can be deflected much easier by two Posse Members than one.

5. After Posse Buddies are established, a discussion of general and specific indecencies occurring within the Posse's neighborhood should highlight how such indecencies are destroying the fabric of the Homeland and what the Posse should do to address and stamp out those indecencies. For instance, if it is known that a neighbor's lawn is being converted to "natural" indigenous plants and that said neighbor has posted a lawn sign saying "We Are Chemical Free," Posse Members could plan to pay a friendly visit to explain the beauty of green manicured lawns. They also could explain how a neighborhood with green manicured lawns looks orderly, controlled, and on alert to outside forces, while a "natural" out-of-control lawn looks like an invitation to foreign chaos.

Now that you have held your first Posse Meeting, you are ready to go on patrol. (Posse Patrol does not have to be active. It

---

[51]It is important that all Posse Members look clean and neat, but not so neat and clean as to arouse suspicion of a homosexual agenda.

can be done from your own living room with a pair of binoculars.) If you have to leave your house, be sure to be equipped with Posse tools and dressed in official Posse garb. In some cases, you will be required to hide or skulk in alleys, behind trees, in shrubbery, and underneath windows.

If indecencies are observed, carefully write down names, dates, times of indecencies, actions taken, and results.[52] Determine the level of threat and make a report. Please use the Posse Indecency Report Form (PIRF). Remember: DOHD wants to know everything, no matter how trivial it may seem to you. The slippery slope of indecency is oiled by inaccurate or shoddy reporting. If you have photographs and tape recordings, we want to see and hear them, too.[53]

While on Posse Patrol, keep in mind the following:

A clean Posse is a professional Posse. Each Posse Member should bathe before and after Posse Patrol. Cleanliness is next to decency.

If it looks like a duck, talks like a duck, walks like a duck, does "it" like a duck, votes Green Party, likes Jon Stewart, buys free-range eggs, is childless by choice, and uses a push mower, it's a duck and it must be reported.

---

[52]While it is acceptable to patrol and report on members of your own family, this should be left to more experienced Posse Members who do not have qualms about turning in indecent family members.

[53]Please label all photographs and tape recordings with a description of the indecencies depicted. DOHD agents, while used to all types of Homeland indecencies, like to have a heads-up before seeing something really indecent. DOHD agents are people, too.

THE NDP QUIZ

Do you have what it takes to be a Neighborhood Decency Posse Member? Take the following quiz to find out. Be honest. DOHD knows when you're not, and cheating will trigger a DOHD LookSee at your home or place of business.

NEIGHBORHOOD DECENCY POSSE
INDIVIDUAL DECENCY DETERMINER

When your neighbor's drapes are shut, do you:
1. Feel left out?
2. Want to knock on his door and ask him what he is doing?
3. Call DOHD anonymously and report him?

Who is most likely to go to Hell?
1. College professors from the East Coast.
2. College professors from the West Coast.
3. College professors.

Who would you most like to go to Hell?
1. Activist judges.
2. Hillary Clinton.
3. President Hillary Clinton.

What is "it"?
1. I will pretend I didn't hear that.
2. I feel faint.
3. Hoo hoo.

Who is your favorite President?
1. Ronald Bush.
2. George Reagan.
3. Karl Rove.

If you could add to the Ten Commandments, what would you like a new commandment to say?
1. Thou shalt not do "it" willy-nilly.
2. Thou shalt not keep DOHD from looking at your medical records.
3. Thou shalt not covet a liberal's wife or his goat.

Which of the following is a good reason to carry a concealed weapon in church?
1. God told me to.
2. Satan told me to.
3. Charlton Heston told me to.

What would make the Homeland more decent? Select all that would apply.
1. Having the Ten Commandments everywhere, including McDonald's.
2. Bombing all Arabs until they give us free gas every Tuesday.
3. Reminding women that we are marching backwards to the future.

4. Exploding condoms.
5. Revamping PBS to include *The O'Reilly Factor*.

What country should be added to the Axis of Evil?
1. France.
2. Canada.
3. Vermont.

Your signature _____

Address _____

Race: White _____ Other _____

Sex: Male _____ Other _____

Please put this form in an envelope, along with $25 to cover the costs of processing, and mail to DOHD.

HOW TO REPORT INDECENCY TO DOHD

DOHD officially recognizes three **Indecency Threat Levels (ITL)**. Before filing a report, a Posse Member must determine the level of threat in his particular situation.

Indecency Threat Level I

This is the lowest-level threat, but it is still reportable. You might have an uneasy feeling about the *Mother Jones* magazine on your neighbor's coffee table, but you're not quite sure if it means anything because they still own two SUVs and drive one of them to church every Sunday. ITLIs cause mild discomfort and suspicion but are not full-blown threats.

Indecency Threat Level II

A medium risk to the Homeland Decency, it is cause for a modicum of alarm. Using the neighbor from above, you notice a second *Mother Jones* magazine on the coffee table, this time dog-eared in three places. One SUV has been replaced by a used Volkswagen and they walk to church. ITLIIs can turn into IIIs at any moment.

Indecency Threat Level III

High Risk to the Homeland Decency! Your neighbor now subscribes to *Mother Jones, The Nation*, and the *Village Voice*; the other SUV is sold; they bicycle to a Unitarian church; they've replaced their lawn with wild flowers and grasses; and one of their sons is too nicely groomed to be heterosexual. ITLIIIs must be reported immediately—before you, the rest of your neighbors, your city, state, and Homeland become infected and die.

Following is a generic PIRF and instructions on how to use it. One Posse Member can make a difference!

POSSE INDECENCY REPORT FORM

Please use ink when filling out this form. Do not leave ANY blank spaces. If you leave a blank space, a DOHD official will need to investigate why you did not fill in all the blanks after being instructed to do so. This causes more work and more stress for DOHD employees who need to spend their time protecting the decency of the Homeland and not worrying why one of their citizens suspiciously neglected to report in a complete manner. In some cases, an incomplete filing will trigger a LookSee.

Name

Last: _____

First: _____

Middle: _____

Maiden: _____

Names from other marriages: _____

Nicknames: _____

Posse name: _____

Marital Status

Single: _____

Married: _____ How many times? _____

Divorced: _____ How many times? _____

Living in sin
(please be specific in terms of time and with whom):

_____

_____

Number of children: _____ Lots _____ None

Sexual orientation: _____ Normal _____ Other

Religious affiliation: _____ Christian _____ Other

Political affiliation: ＿＿＿＿ Republican ＿＿＿ Other

Do you own a gun? ＿＿＿＿ Of course

If you are not a white American, what are you? ＿＿＿＿＿＿

Address

Street: ＿＿＿＿＿＿＿＿＿ Apt#: ＿＿＿＿＿＿＿＿

City: ＿＿＿＿＿＿＿＿＿ State: ＿＿＿＿＿＿＿＿

Zip code: ＿＿＿＿＿＿＿＿＿＿＿＿＿＿＿＿＿＿

Kind of place you live in (home, apartment, condo, town house, trailer, tent, commune—be specific): ＿＿＿＿＿＿＿＿＿

Phone Number

Work: ＿＿＿＿＿＿＿＿＿ Home: ＿＿＿＿＿＿＿

Cell: ＿＿＿＿＿＿＿＿＿

Phone numbers of your children: ＿＿＿＿＿＿＿＿＿

Phone numbers of two of your closest friends: ＿＿＿＿＿＿

E-mail

E-mail address: ＿＿＿＿＿＿＿＿＿＿＿＿＿＿＿＿

E-mail addresses of your children: ＿＿＿＿＿＿＿＿

E-mail addresses of two of your closest friends: ＿＿＿＿＿

Last twenty websites you visited and why:

Whom are you reporting?

Name: _____

Address: _____

Phone number: _____

Cell: _____

E-mail address: _____

Work address: _____

Work phone number: _____

When did you first view the possible threat to Homeland Decency? (check one)

___ Morning ___ Afternoon

___ Evening ___ Middle of the night

___ I didn't actually see it. My Posse Buddy did and told me about it.

What method did you use to detect the possible threat to Homeland Decency?

___ Eyes only ___ Binoculars

___ Binoculars and tape recorder

___ Binoculars, tape recorder, and camera

Was the subject aware of your detection?

____ Yes, and he/she was upset.

____ Yes, and he/she didn't care.

____ Yes, and I had to draw my gun.

Where did you detect the possible threat?

____ In the home.

    Where?

    ____ Medicine cabinet ____ Under the bed ____ Other

____ In the workplace.

    Where?

    ____ Desk ____ Computer screen

    ____ In the bathroom when I looked under the stall.

What are you reporting? Please be specific:

_____

_____

_____

Was unnatural nudity or "it" involved? Be specific: _____

_____

If we initiate a DOHD LookSee of this individual, will you and your Posse Buddy be available to back us up?

____ Yes. We like confrontation when it's for the good of the Homeland.

____ No. We would like to remain anonymous so we can continue our work as spies for the Homeland.

____ Maybe. If you're using guns, we might be interested.

Have you ever done "it" out of wedlock?[54]

____ No. Never. I am a Posse Member!

____ Yes, and I have suffered from a lifetime of sores.[55]

Your signature _____

Date _____

Please put this form in an envelope, along with $25 to cover the costs of processing, and mail to DOHD. We might contact you before our LookSee, and we might not.

---

[54]This question might not seem relevant to a Posse Indecency Report, but you have to trust us that it is and that we need to know all that stuff about you.
[55]A DOHD trick question. We need to be sure you didn't lie on your Posse Individual Decency Determiner.

Fun facts to teach your kids:

Doing "it" is evil.

Terrorists do "it" all the time
and have sores.

Condoms can explode.

FUND-RAISING FOR HOMELAND DECENCY

DOHD gets its funding from the Congress of the United States under the UDA. But it could use your help. While rooting out and punishing indecency is the top priority of the Homeland, some years are leaner than others. It depends on who is leading the Homeland, the makeup of the Congress, and what foreign wars against indecency we are currently engaged in. That is why we encourage all decent Homeland citizens to proactively find creative ways to make money to help DOHD.

Following are a few suggestions for DOHD fund-raisers that have worked for some citizens. Use your imagination. The possibilities are limited only by your decency.

Remember, once you have held your DOHD fund-raiser, you must send your money to DOHD immediately. DOHD will then funnel that money back into decency projects, including Neighborhood Decency Posse Grants; new equipment for

DOHD SUVs; establishment of indecency detention centers and indecency examiners; benefits for DOHD employees; our GAG Bible Placement Program; "it" abstinence pamphlets; condom-burning efforts; and the like. As always, the money you earn means our march backwards to the future is shorter! That means fewer blisters for all of us!

ABSTINENCE BAKE SALE

What says "decency" more than a bake sale? It requires little more than a few flyers and decent women who feel it is important to bake for the DOHD abstinence cause. Make your bake sale different from the run-of-the-mill version by hiding clever messages in the baked goods. Tweens and teens are sure to love biting into a chocolate-chip cookie and finding Abstinence Fortunes like the following:

- Doing "it" is evil.
- Terrorists do "it" all the time and have sores.
- Condoms can explode.

Try to bake cakes and cookies in interesting shapes, like crucifixes, the flag, or the President's head.

TRADITIONAL MARRIAGE 10K AND FUN RUN

This is a wonderful opportunity to make money and show how the traditional family that runs together stays together. Traditional married couples running in pairs along the Homeland roadways is a model and inspiration for all those (including OHFs) who stand on the sidelines to cheer them on. While the 10K is for married adults, the Fun Run is for children who support their parents and who have signed pledges not to do "it" until after marriage. Have runners circulate pledge forms that encourage people to support them through the physical miles of the 10K and the spiritual miles of the 10K of marriage. Extra money can be made with T-shirt and hat sales. Sample messages might include the following:

- If God had wanted Bob and Bob to get married,
  He wouldn't have made wedding gowns.
- If God had wanted Betty and Betty to get married,
  He wouldn't have made stag parties.
- Boycott Canada and Spain!

OHF couples who are going through "changeback counseling" may be allowed to run at the back of the race.

FAITH-BASED SCIENCE AND TECHNOLOGY FAIRS

People of faith no longer need to avoid science. And their children can now enjoy many of the benefits of school science fairs without a terrifying challenge to their faith.

Have your school hold a Faith-Based Science and Technology Fair. These exciting competitions place as high a value on faith as on scientific knowledge. The winners of these often have their inventions manufactured and sold, with a portion of the profits going to DOHD.

The past two years have seen the development of the following products that have raised big funds for DOHD.

FAITH-BASED TOASTER. A team of decent, young, faith-based scientists theorized that computer chips placed in toasters could be programmed to pick up brain waves. They programmed a chip to read these auras and then burn the toast of secular humanists and atheists[56] but not of the faithful. The toast of the faithful popped up perfect every time.

FAITH-BASED DOORBELLS. An eight-year-old faith-based scientist theorized that there was a difference in the galvanic skin response of virgins and nonvirgins when they visited people of faith and programmed a computer chip to read this. This chip was put in a doorbell and programmed so the bell would ring only for virgins. Nonvirgins received a small electrical shock, suggesting that they were not welcome at this house until they changed their ways.[57]

DECENCY OLYMPICS

Games are wholesome. Competitive games that make money for DOHD are even more wholesome. Here's a fun way to learn

---

[56]A DOHD investigation found no connection between 1,500 house fires and the regular use of faith-based toasters.

[57]A DOHD investigation found no connection between the electrocutions of twenty-seven alleged virgins and the installation of this doorbell.

about decency, link it to terrorism, and make money at the same time: Your neighborhood can form teams to play other neighborhoods, using a variety of terrorist-related strategy games. The DOHD publishes a list of approved games (e.g., Three-Legged Axis of Evil Sack Race, and Capture the Terrorist and Save the Virgin) on its website.

PLEASE NOTE

While DOHD does not condone gambling, when wagering is done to aid DOHD and its enforcement of the USA DECENCY ACT, then it is acceptable. DOHD will accept any monies garnered from fund-raising casino nights, horse racing, charity cockfights, bingo, and football pools.

Monies earned by fund-raising for Homeland Decency and sent to DOHD are not tax-deductible, because that would make the Homeland poorer and thus weaker.

You need only to turn to one of our
leading television networks to see that
blond newswomen are not only more
fair and balanced but also seem
to be having more fun.

HOMELAND EXTRA-INTERVENTION

What does a decent Homelander do in situations not covered in this handbook? Or if they spot something indecent and dangerous and their Neighborhood Decency Posse is busy on some other important mission? DOHD wants you—the eyes and ears of Homeland Decency—to be unafraid to report an incident or situation in which you feel DOHD might have purview, even though it might seem outside of it. If DOHD can assist in eradicating a threat to the Homeland, it will do so.

You are now acquainted with the most common concerns of DOHD. But some sitations are not black and white. We place these concerns in the category of Extra-Intervention—concerns outside the normal DOHD issues (e.g., handling "it," one-Mommy-one-Daddy traditional marriages, anti-Homeland lawn signage). The following examples give you some idea of the situations you might encounter. They will remind you to keep your eyes and ears open to a much wider range of threat possibilities. As always, we welcome all your questions and concerns.

Q: *I am very concerned about one of our local news stations. Unlike other news stations, this one uses a brunette news anchor and she does not laugh very much when she delivers the news. I have always been taught that brunette women are more liberal, don't laugh much, and probably do "it" a little too often. Is this a situation DOHD can do something about?*

A: You have every right to be concerned about this. You need only to turn to one of our leading television networks to see that blond newswomen not only are more fair and balanced but also seem to be having more fun. While they probably do "it," they most likely don't do "it" as often as brunettes. And when they do do "it," it is with their husbands in the Homeland Way. As far as an extra-intervention in this case, we feel it is much better if you begin a local letter-writing campaign to this particular station. Tell them your concerns. Make sure they understand that the delivery of news is much better performed by someone with a cheerful and moral attitude. Tell them you are depressed by her news delivery and that you want to feel uplifted after a report on your government's plans to, say, bring democracy to another indecent emirate. If this fails, DOHD can help you partner with the FCC and some select faith-based organizations for additional clout.

Q: *Is steroid use anti-Homeland?*

A: DOHD is still studying this issue in concert with the FDA and several major drug companies. Many large corporations like to be associated with winning teams: It inspires generosity. Being "strong," and thus contributing to his team's winning season, is also a fine way for a not-white to pull himself up by the bootstraps. And winning is a wonderful value to teach our young people. But you can see the problem. These young people grow up to become professional athletes and—while providing wonderful revenue for television networks and hours of healthy entertainment for the Homeland—become very wealthy, haughty, and do "it" outside the confines of marriage. At this point, DOHD is trying to balance the need for a winning team attitude and the goal of a drug-free Homeland.

Q: *What should I do about a neighbor who never buys anything new? While I am not against recycling (even though it seems like a liberal idea), isn't it possible that too much recycling is not a good thing for the Homeland? My neighbor—who, by the way, has a good job and makes quite a bit of money—always buys used cars, shops at secondhand clothing and furniture stores, and even brings back her grocery bags to the grocery store so they can be used again. What, if anything, should I do about this?*

A: While recycling was probably started by liberals, we at DOHD have always been on board—until recently. Recycling cans, bottles, and newspapers is fine. Buying used cars is dangerous. One reason our Homeland is strong is that we produce new things and people buy them. If people stop purchasing new things like SUVs, the backbone of our Homeland—large manufacturers—becomes brittle and weak. Without a strong backbone, the Homeland becomes prey to large foreign manufacturers with strange and unhealthy ideas about morality. You can see what a slippery slope this can be. If you buy a lot of used merchandise, people in other countries (like France, where doing "it" is a normal part of the day, like drinking wine) start to look more stylish, drive better cars, and sit on nicer couches than we do. A strong Homeland is a brand-spanking-new and sparkly Homeland, not a rusty, threadbare Homeland. We suggest you continue to buy new things and make a point of showing off your new things to your neighbors. If you fail to impress them, we have ways of impressing them that, while maybe not legal, are relatively painless.

Q: *I feel funny about houses that don't display Christmas lights during Christmas. Why is that?*

A: You are probably observing homes that contain people of non-Christian faith or those who are too lazy to decorate their homes for the Christmas season. DOHD, while respecting all religious beliefs, believes that everyone understands that the Homeland is based on Christian values. Santa Claus and Jesus are just as crucial to a value-based Homeland as marriage and meat loaf. DOHD suggests applying enough pressure—with other neighbors or using letters to the editor with a somewhat specific location of the offending home—to at least put up one string of lights. When an entire block of homes is decorated, it says to the terrorists: "We're inside and Jesus is outside! Just try to break in!"

Q: *I agree with DOHD's insistence that English should be the language of everyone who lives in this country. So I am uncomfortable with my children having to learn another language in school. If they are forced to take French, I worry they will start talking only in French and then start behaving like French people. If there is no way I can stop my child from having to learn another language, is there one language that is better and safer to learn than another?*

A: DOHD is adamant that English be the first and only language of the Homeland. If you wish to speak another language, you are absolutely free to go live in the country where that language is spoken. That's what makes our Homeland such a great place.

DOHD intends to sponsor an "I Only Talk English" bill that will require all citizens of the Homeland to speak English at all times, even in their own homes. The bill will also relieve all those agencies/businesses—governmental and private—of the burden of having to cater to non-English-speaking residents. It will also put an end to multilingual instruction manuals.

You are right to be concerned about your child being forced to become bilingual. The rest of the world must become accustomed to the idea that the Homeland is still the leader of all that is moral and decent. Until things change, schools can still require your children to take a second language. You may not have a choice in the language they study. If you are given a choice, try not to choose French—for obvious reasons that have been expressed many times in this handbook.

Q: *Ratings for movies is a good idea. But I think we could do even more. We rate movies for "it" and violence and swearing. But what about movies that are anti-Homeland? Shouldn't we have a rating that says whether or not a movie promotes the values of the Homeland? A movie without "it," violence, and swearing can still be dangerous. Is it possible for DOHD to become involved in this?*

A: DOHD not only agrees with you but is about to release its findings in a special report titled "The Homeland Rating System: How to Make Hollywood HOLYwood." A copy of this report can be obtained from DOHD.

In the meantime, DOHD has always maintained a list of movies that we feel promote and extol the values of the Homeland and those that don't. The movies are rated thusly:

PH (pro-Homeland)

AH (anti-Homeland)

AHI (anti-Homeland with lots of scenes of "it")

AHLI (anti-Homeland with lots of language about "it")

AHFI (anti-Homeland with the American flag shown in scenes of "it")

AHCI (anti-Homeland with "it" happening anywhere near a church)

AHGI (anti-Homeland with "it" happening anywhere near a government building)

AHSI (anti-Homeland with "it" happening anywhere near a school)

AHAPI (anti-Homeland with "it" happening anywhere near an apple pie)

DOHD is currently working on similar ratings lists for books and music.

Q: *I have religiously used my leaf blower every fall. It does a very good job. My neighbors use a rake. When they are finished, there are still small leaf scraps on their lawns. They are angry with me for using the leaf blower and say that I am in favor of air and noise pollution. I say it is more important to have a clean, leaf-free lawn and that using a rake says you only half care about your Homeland's appearance. Is there something I can do about this? And does DOHD have a policy addressing people who don't spray for dandelions and insects? And those who don't immediately pick up their dog's poop?*

A: You are a good Homeland neighbor. And you are right. If we don't look like we have control over our own yards, what terrorist would be afraid of opening up our front doors and waltzing right into our living rooms, sitting down on our couches, and grabbing the remote? A pristine yard in a neighborhood of pristine yards is a safe and decent place for the Homeland's children to play without fear of bugs, dandelion stains, and animal waste.

Before DOHD intervenes, it wants you to try a few things. After the first leaves fall, very early in the morning, rev up your leaf blower and clean your lawn and those on either side of you.

You might be surprised at your neighbors' reactions. Most people who own rakes hate raking. Plus, DOHD believes these neighbors are probably more jealous than angry, because most real Homeland men cannot resist large gas-powered tools of any kind.

When it comes to weed/insect control and eradication, DOHD suggests you wait for a windy day to tend to your dandelion/bug spray plan. The wind will carry any chemical you employ into the adjoining yards, again saving your neighbors the time and the trouble of doing it themselves.

DOHD does not pick up poop and consequently does not intervene in lawn waste issues.

ADDRESS ALL ADDITIONAL HOMELAND DECENCY CONCERNS TO DOHD. THE FIRST THREE QUESTIONS ARE FREE. EACH ADDITIONAL QUESTION WILL BE ANSWERED FOR $3.95. DIRECT DOHD INTERVENTION IS ADDITIONAL AND DEPENDS ON THE DIFFICULTY AND LEVEL OF PERIL TO THE HOMELAND.

INDECENT QUESTIONS MAY TRIGGER A LOOKSEE.

THE EXTRA-INTERVENTION LIST IS UPDATED EVERY WEEK. IT IS UP TO YOU TO REMAIN INFORMED AND VIGILANT.